Body Piercing
and Tattoos

Other Books in the Social Issues Firsthand Series:

SOCIAL ISSUES
FIRSTHAND

Body Piercing and Tattoos

Stefan Kiesbye, Book Editor

GREENHAVEN PRESS
A part of Gale, Cengage Learning

GALE
CENGAGE Learning

Detroit • New York • San Francisco • New Haven, Conn • Waterville, Maine • London

Christine Nasso, *Publisher*
Elizabeth Des Chenes, *Managing Editor*

© 2009 Greenhaven Press, a part of Gale, Cengage Learning.

Gale and Greenhaven Press are registered trademarks used herein under license.

For more information, contact:
Greenhaven Press
27500 Drake Rd.
Farmington Hills, MI 48331-3535
Or you can visit our Internet site at gale.cengage.com

For product information and technology assistance, contact us at

Gale Customer Support, 1-800-877-4253
For permission to use material from this text or product, submit all requests online at www.cengage.com/permissions

Further permissions questions can be emailed to permissionrequest@cengage.com

Articles in Greenhaven Press anthologies are often edited for length to meet page requirements. In addition, original titles of these works are changed to clearly present the main thesis and to explicitly indicate the author's opinion. Every effort is made to ensure that Greenhaven Press accurately reflects the original intent of the authors. Every effort has been made to trace the owners of copyrighted material.

Cover image copyright iofoto, 2008. Used under license from Shutterstock.com.

LIBRARY OF CONGRESS CATALOGING-IN-PUBLICATION DATA

Body piercing and tattoos / Stefan Kiesbye, book editor.
    p. cm. -- (Social issues firsthand)
    Includes bibliographical references and index.
    ISBN 978-0-7377-4249-7 (hardcover)
    1. Body piercing. 2. Tattooing. I. Kiesbye, Stefan.
    GN419.25.B62 2009
    391.6'5--dc22
                                 2008026080

Printed in the United States of America
1 2 3 4 5 6 7 12 11 10 09 08

Contents

Chapter 2: Health and Social Issues

Chapter 3: Piercing and Tattoo Artists at Work

Foreword

Social issues are often viewed in abstract terms. Pressing challenges such as poverty, homelessness, and addiction are viewed as problems to be defined and solved. Politicians, social scientists, and other experts engage in debates about the extent of the problems, their causes, and how best to remedy them. Often overlooked in these discussions is the human dimension of the issue. Behind every policy debate over poverty, homelessness, and substance abuse, for example, are real people struggling to make ends meet, to survive life on the streets, and to overcome addiction to drugs and alcohol. Their stories are ubiquitous and compelling. They are the stories of everyday people—perhaps your own family members or friends—and yet they rarely influence the debates taking place in state capitols, the national Congress, or the courts.

The disparity between the public debate and private experience of social issues is well illustrated by looking at the topic of poverty. Each year the U.S. Census Bureau establishes a poverty threshold. A household with an income below the threshold is defined as poor, while a household with an income above the threshold is considered able to live on a basic subsistence level. For example, in 2003 a family of two was considered poor if its income was less than $12,015; a family of four was defined as poor if its income was less than $18,810. Based on this system, the bureau estimates that 35.9 million Americans (12.5 percent of the population) lived below the poverty line in 2003, including 12.9 million children below the age of eighteen.

Commentators disagree about what these statistics mean. Social activists insist that the huge number of officially poor Americans translates into human suffering. Even many families that have incomes above the threshold, they maintain, are likely to be struggling to get by. Other commentators insist that the statistics exaggerate the problem of poverty in the United States. Compared to people in developing countries, they point out, most so-called poor families have a high quality of life. As stated by journalist Fidelis Iyebote, "Cars are owned by 70 percent of 'poor' households. . . . Color televisions belong to 97 percent of the 'poor' [and] videocassette recorders belong to nearly 75 percent. . . . Sixty-four percent have microwave ovens, half own a stereo system, and over a quarter possess an automatic dishwasher."

However, this debate over the poverty threshold and what it means is likely irrelevant to a person living in poverty. Simply put, poor people do not need the government to tell them whether they are poor. They can see it in the stack of bills they cannot pay. They are aware of it when they are forced to choose between paying rent or buying food for their children. They become painfully conscious of it when they lose their homes and are forced to live in their cars or on the streets. Indeed, the written stories of poor people define the meaning of poverty more vividly than a government bureaucracy could ever hope to. Narratives composed by the poor describe losing jobs due to injury or mental illness, depict horrific tales of childhood abuse and spousal violence, recount the loss of friends and family members. They evoke the slipping away of social supports and government assistance, the descent into substance abuse and addiction, the harsh realities of life on the streets. These are the perspectives on poverty that are too often omitted from discussions over the extent of the problem and how to solve it.

Greenhaven Press's *Social Issues Firsthand* series provides a forum for the often-overlooked human perspectives on society's most divisive topics of debate. Each volume focuses on one social issue and presents a collection of ten to sixteen narratives by those who have had personal involvement with the topic. Extra care has been taken to include a diverse range of perspectives. For example, in the volume on adoption, readers will find the stories of birth parents who have made an adoption plan, adoptive parents, and adoptees themselves. After exposure to these varied points of view, the reader will have a clearer understanding that adoption is an intense, emotional experience full of joyous highs and painful lows for all concerned.

The debate surrounding embryonic stem cell research illustrates the moral and ethical pressure that the public brings to bear on the scientific community. However, while nonexperts often criticize scientists for not considering the potential negative impact of their work, ironically the public's reaction against such discoveries can produce harmful results as well. For example, although the outcry against embryonic stem cell research in the United States has resulted in fewer embryos being destroyed, those with Parkinson's, such as actor Michael J. Fox, have argued that prohibiting the development of new stem cell lines ultimately will prevent a timely cure for the disease that is killing Fox and thousands of others.

Each book in the series contains several features that enhance its usefulness, including an in-depth introduction, an annotated table of contents, bibliographies for further research, a list of organizations to contact, and a thorough index. These elements—combined with the poignant voices of people touched by tragedy and triumph—make the *Social Issues Firsthand* series a valuable resource for research on today's topics of political discussion.

Introduction

"I've spent most of my life feeling uncomfortable. Uncomfortable with myself, with other people, in public and in private. I grew up knowing that something was missing, that something was not right," says Frances Sand in a statement on the Web site *Modified Mind*. Her way of finding herself might seem unusual to many. Over the years Sand has been tattooed and pierced many times, and also chose to get implants under her skin. Pictures of her show facial tattoos and piercing of her nose and ears, forehead and lower lip. Her subdermal implants are visible on her arm. "I never saw myself as showing any kind of bravery, this was not a conscious decision for me. All I knew was that it didn't feel wrong to me, and that as I grew older and those feelings that I was harming myself in some way faded away as being insignificant, something in all of this was building the person I was to become."

While many people regard tattoos and piercing as a fad, a mere fashion trend that will fade as quickly as bell bottoms or shoulder pads, Sand touches on the notion that tattoos can be an expression of self and spirituality. The ubiquitous lower-back tattoo, or the legion of butterflies and unicorns might one day be the cause for regret for many, but people like Sand and Jason Abels have found fulfillment in body modification. Abels is a minister in the Church of Body Modification. Interviewed by *Modified Mind*, he says, "Ever since I can remember I have been a deeply spiritual person. My relationship with God is what my life is built around, and the foundation for my very being. Because of this I felt it was only natural to incorporate it into my designs and plans for my appearance. Even before I started getting tattooed I had branded and cut Christian imagery onto my arms and shoulders. I had performed my first deep, permanent cutting on myself when I was 15 to commemorate the anniversary of my baptism and because that was the year that I really found my relationship with my Lord. Once that cutting faded I branded over it."

Abels has "15 piercings (4 of them dermal punched, the rest pierced), a decent amount of tattoo coverage, 2 implants, 3 large cuttings and a number of smaller cuttings and brandings. I also have . . . a split tongue," he said, among other modifications.

For Sand and Abels, body modifications go far beyond adornment or the short-lived wish to be cool. The practices are integral to their being and become means to connect with a sense of self and that of a higher realm.

But most churches do not encourage tattoos. Rabbi Alan B. Lucas of Temple Beth Shalom in Roslyn Heights, New York, writes that, "Tattooing is an explicit prohibition from the Torah. However, those who violate this prohibition may be buried in a Jewish cemetery and participate fully in all synagogue ritual. While no sanctions are imposed, the practice should continue to be discouraged as a violation of the Torah."

Dr. Muzammil Siddiqi, former president of the Islamic Society of North America, is quoted on the IslamOnline Web site, saying that, "it is [unlawful] to have tattoos on the body. However, the Prophet (peace and blessings be upon him) is reported to have said, 'Islam takes away the sins done before it.'" In his opinion, tattoos are no reason to deny new converts who got tattoos previously. According to the Web site, only the piercing of ears is allowed for women.

Father John Matusiak of the Orthodox Church in America, asked about his church's view on tattoos and piercing, states that, "There is nothing, at least to my knowledge (which is somewhat limited), in the Holy Fathers on such matters, and I do not believe that any hierarch or Synod has addressed this currently popular practice. . . . The Church has always warned against undue concern for one's appearance or undue concern for calling attention to the self, especially when doing so becomes obsession and, therefore, a sin. . . . I would say that any discussion on the matter of piercing and tattoos would have to involve the following elements: Why did the person choose to have the piercing or tattoos—as a 'fashion statement' or as a means of self mutilation. . . . Are they likely to become a stumbling block or obstacle between a person and his/her relationship with Christ and the People of God?"

Matusiak's opinion is echoed by Brother John-Paul Ignatius Mary of the Order of the Legion of St. Michael in Iowa, quoted in a *Catholic Register* article as saying, "Ostentatious displays and decorations are generally not consistent with Christian modesty and decorum and as Christians we are to be modest and to avoid vanity and pride."

Sand and Abels don't understand body modification as mutilation, and Abels dispels the notion that he wants to draw attention to himself. "I have the name of God written on my face in Hebrew and the word 'Forgiven' across my knuckles for this reason. I don't want my tattoos to shock or disturb, I just want to cause people to think about the things they represent. . . . You can take off a Christian shirt, and you can remove a WWJD [What Would Jesus Do?] bracelet or cross necklace when you don't want to portray yourself as different, but I cannot do this with my mod[ification]s. They act as a reminder to me and to others that I am not my own, but that I am a servant of God, and should act accordingly. It also serves as a reminder of the sacrifice that was made to atone for my sins and the redemption and forgiveness that I have through Christ," he said.

Social Issues Firsthand: Body Piercing and Tattoos presents personal narratives from a number of perspectives, focusing on the experience of getting pierced or tattooed, the health and social issues involved, and the experiences of artists and others working in the body modification industry. The following viewpoints demonstrate a variety of perspectives and provide a catalyst for further discussion.

CHAPTER 1

Getting a Body Piercing or Tattoo

A Disabled Man Defines His Identity Through Piercing and Tattoos

Adam Cline

The author—diagnosed with a rare form of muscular dystrophy, Friedreich's ataxia—describes how body art and body modifications give him a sense of autonomy he rarely feels in everyday routines. Because his illness makes him appear mentally disabled, he shows through piercing and brandings that he does not conform to society's expectations of people with disabilities.

My body continues to change—I continue to define my identity. Wheelchair or no wheelchair. I now have new piercings, more ink, a branding and more to come. . . . Everybody asks 'Why.' Do I hate my body enough to mutilate it? Or do I love it enough to celebrate and decorate it? I can't give a clear answer.

My disability more or less forces me to be conscious of my identity. Therefore, my disability has become a large contributor to who I am. My lack of muscle control, my speech impediment, my physical breakdown have shaped my identity. My mental capacities largely exist in what forms they may because of my physical capacities. I think as a man on the outskirts of society because the handicapped will never be incorporated into the mainstream. Therefore, I have reclaimed my body through physical adornment because, for me, this act coincides with my mentality. I have pierced and tattooed myself, my body, to complement my disability. Body art gives me a new way of looking at myself. Anyway, I figure if people are gonna stare because of the chair—I might as well give them something interesting to look at. A chair by itself is pretty boring.

Adam Cline, "Defining My Identity Through the Outside from the Inside," *Modified Mind*, August 11, 2007. http://modifiedmind.com. Reproduced by permission.

Fighting Wrong Perceptions

Tattooing and piercing provide me with an unspoken language in which to define myself. Because of my speech problems, along with my disability, people assume that I am mentally retarded. The body art, however, is a way to show people that I can think for myself. I mean, let's face it, no parent in their right mind would tattoo their child. My body art provides me with a clear voice I may otherwise not have. I can now clearly show the world who (or what) I am.

Because of my dependence on others to provide me with aid in bathing, dressing, almost all actions largely taken for granted by the abled; I feel my body is no longer my own. I need help in almost every physical aspect of my life. People can, a lot of times, choose my bedtime, choose my clothing, among other things—I feel very limited. But with piercing and tattooing I make the choice of what happens to my body. This way I reclaim my body as my own. Also, my disability is caused by a degenerative muscle disease, muscular dystrophy, that causes my current physical condition to be temporary, ever changing. My body art is permanent; it will always be there. My tattooing and piercing provide a sense of stability in their permanence.

Assimilation Seems Impossible

Other disabled individuals, by and large, have attempted assimilation into the social mainstream. I strongly believe that no matter what, the disabled will never be part of the mainstream—never be "normal." Anyway, normal is boring. I personally have chosen to go the other way and remove myself from the mainstream (or that possibility) as much as possible. I'm already seen as different from the norm because of my disability—a physical deviation. The "physical norm" in this country belongs to the abled. Anything outside that norm is seen by most as freakish. I choose to take that "freakishness" and complement it with body piercing and tattooing.

I understand the point that other disabled individuals are trying to make by being as "normal" as possible. They are attempting total assimilation by wearing clothes, listening to music, and so on, that conform to the social mainstream. When many of the disabled people see me they are angered. They look at me as though I were rubbing salt on the wound. I am seen as a contra in the battle for the assimilation of persons with disabilities. But I feel their way is counterproductive, a backslide. We need to thrust our individuality to the front lines.

Disabled People Are Expected to Conform

I remember, when I used to wear my hair in a Mohawk, I passed two women who commented; "There's something you don't see every day—a handicapped person with a Mohawk." Why is that? I guess people just don't expect the handicapped to go against the grain. But it's idiotic people like these two women that make me want to go against the grain in the worst way. I don't want others to assume what my identity should be because of my disability. The assumption is widespread that the disabled largely do not go against the grain. People expect the disabled to conform.

As my disability largely defines my identity, I am also not going to let it define me on its own. For instance, I will not change who I am because of my disability. My disability is not the sole reason I'm into body art. A freak is a freak is a freak. I would be even more heavily pierced and tattooed, but my disability prevents me from tattooing or piercing certain parts of my body. The possibility of a career also prevents such action. My parents always say that it's hard enough for me to get a job because of my disability, but my body art only makes matters worse. They also believe strongly that it is difficult for me to integrate into society fully because of the disability and they believe my body art only adds to the problem. But I figure people need to get over it—both the disability and the body art. That goes for everyone.

In the same sense my disability has not become the main voice throughout my writing. Out of hundreds of poems I have maybe five that have a theme of disability. Which is strange because my disability is in the forefront of most other aspects of my life. I do have a few poems about body art. Body art has provided a stronger voice with which to write. Perhaps, though, my body art is used to subconsciously mask my disability throughout my writing.

Reclaiming Individuality

I was diagnosed with a fairly rare form of muscular dystrophy, Friedreich's ataxia, when I was seven. This meant that I would have to wear leg braces and a back brace. This "oddity" would be seen clearly by my peers. Part of me welcomed this oddity with open arms; I could now be physically different—more of an individual. As I entered high school and the wheelchair, however, I wanted to be like everyone else. I hated my disability. My comfort with my disability came later in life. I became comfortable with my difference. Body art gives me the power to choose—to reclaim my difference as my own.

My first tattoo came when I had just turned twenty. Eight years later I am up to something like seventeen (some are "blended" together). I now have only three piercings; one in my right rook (cartilage right above the ear canal), one conch, and a vertical nipple. I have had well over twenty facial piercings. I also have a brand of the infinity symbol on my right forearm. What's next? You'll have to wait and see. . . .

Overall, I do this to overshadow my disability for myself and others. People focus on the body art and don't think about the disability for a moment. Or, maybe, it's the other way around; perhaps the body art brings more focus to the disability. I don't know or really care anymore. People are going to look at me however they want. So, for that reason, I will be the biggest FREAK I want.

Piercing as a Symbol of a Young Woman's Independence

Anonymous

A teenager, trying to step out of the shadows of her parents, gets pierced in secret and against the wishes of her mother. The ensuing healing process, marked by episodes of intense pain, becomes a metaphor for gaining independence and for dealing with difficult decisions on her own.

Ever since I was a freshman, I'd wanted to get my navel pierced. I think navel rings look cute the way they dangle over the belly button, and come in so many styles and colors.

By the time I was a junior, I'd become obsessed with the idea. One afternoon when my mom was sitting in the kitchen reading the paper, I asked her, "Mommy, can I get a tattoo?" I didn't really want a tattoo. I just wanted to see her reaction before I asked her the real question.

"No, you can't get a tattoo," she said. "Are you crazy?"

I laughed and told her that I was only joking. Then I said, "Mommy, can I get a piercing?"

For a minute she didn't answer me. Then she said, "What do you want pierced?"

"My belly button."

Again she hesitated. "No, not right now. Wait until you're about to leave for college," she told me. "That way your father won't go ballistic and try to kill you."

I Want to Make My Own Decisions

I didn't press the subject. I'd already decided that if she said no (which I'd expected her to), I was going to get it done anyway. I wanted to prove to myself that I'm not afraid of my parents and am not the type of person who gives in to everything her mother and father say.

If my mom had given me permission to get the piercing, I don't know if I'd have done it. I wouldn't want her watching over me 24-7 asking if I cleaned it or if it's healing properly.

I usually do listen to my parents, but I feel like they're too controlling. I want to make my own decisions and learn from my own mistakes. With the piercing, I wanted to know that I could make a decision that wasn't up to anyone but me. Hidden under my shirt, my pierced navel would be a private symbol of my independence.

Didn't Ask for ID

So on April 4, my friend Carla (not her real name) took me to a place in downtown Brooklyn where she'd gotten one of her two tattoos.

"I'm getting pierced at a cell phone store?" I asked her when I saw the place.

"No, b-tch, it's in the back," she laughed.

The woman at the piercing parlor said it'd cost $35. I wondered what I'd say to her if she asked me to present proper identification. If you're under 18 in New York, you're supposed to have a parent's consent for a piercing.

But she didn't ask me for ID. She told me to pick out a ring, and I chose a silver barbell with a crystal diamond. It reflected beautifully in the light. I thought about it shining in the sun while I lay on the beach.

The woman at the parlor said, "Wait a few minutes."

Is the Needle Clean?

That's when I became nervous. "Suppose she doesn't use a clean needle? What if I don't get pierced properly and it gets infected?" I thought about leaving, but I knew I'd regret it later. Plus, I'd already given her my $35.

A few minutes later, she told me to come with her into a small blue room with a dentist's chair. By this time I was so nervous I felt like I was going to pass out.

She closed the door and slipped on a pair of gloves. "Lie back and unbutton your jeans," she said. When I did, she took an alcohol pad and wiped the area above my navel.

I made sure to watch her every move to see that she was being careful and using a new needle. I knew that I could get a disease or infection from a previously used needle. So I was relieved when she pulled a fresh needle out of a wrapper.

I Wanted to Scream

Then I saw that the needle was about six inches long. I had to close my eyes. I didn't want to see that thing getting pushed inside my stomach like I was a piece of cloth.

I felt the needle go in, and it wasn't too bad. It was when she was trying to get it to come out of the top that was the problem. It was like she was forcing the needle out and it hurt like crazy. I wanted to scream, but I didn't want to look stupid.

After the needle came out, she took the ring and placed it inside the hole. It was finally over.

I didn't even look at the piercing to see how it turned out. I was kind of in shock. I couldn't believe that I had a needle stuck through my stomach. And I couldn't believe that I'd disobeyed my mom and done something even though she told me not to do it.

But I also felt excited. Just the thrill of doing something so drastic behind my parents' backs, making my own decision for a change, sent chills throughout my body. I immediately wanted to go shopping to buy clothing that would show off my new piercing.

Lumpy and Swollen

When I left the little room, Carla looked at me and started smiling. "Let me see it! Let me see it!"

I lifted my shirt up.

"That's mad cute," Carla said.

Seeing my piercing for the first time, I didn't think it looked cute. It looked lumpy and swollen. "Thanks," I said.

It was $5 more to buy the medicine to clean my piercing. The lady who pierced me didn't explain how to clean and take care of it, but I'd done research about that on the internet. I knew how to clean it and that it'd take four months to a year to heal properly.

Couldn't Sleep on My Stomach

Going home, we had to stand up because the bus was filled with rowdy kids coming home from school. My hand was in front of my stomach the whole time. I was afraid that someone might hit me in my piercing when they moved. I felt like there was blood dripping down my stomach, but my shirt was still clean.

At home, I took out the cleaning solution. It said that it wouldn't burn. But it did. Big time. I had to grab the edge of the sink to keep from screaming.

That night I couldn't sleep on my stomach, the way I was used to, because the piercing irritated me too much.

The next morning it didn't hurt too badly, but when I was getting dressed, I accidentally pushed down on the ring with too much force. "Ow!" I yelped quietly. I felt a pain shoot through the lower part of my stomach.

My Friends Thought I Was Crazy

At school the next Monday, I couldn't wait to show all my friends that I got my navel pierced. I wondered what they'd say. Plus, my friends like to joke around and hit me in the stomach. I didn't want to take that chance; I could just imagine the pain.

They were surprised when I told them I had it done. "Did it hurt?" they asked. "Do your parents know about it?"

When I said no, they all looked at me as if I were crazy. "Do you really think your parents won't find out about it?" they asked.

"I hope not," I said. I explained that at home, I kept the bathroom door locked when taking a shower and wore baggy shirts so that the piercing wasn't revealed.

Over the next few days, I expected my piercing to gradually heal and become less painful. But it didn't. I still couldn't sleep on my stomach or wear button-down shirts because it hurt too much.

Like Caring for a Pet

One day I was joking around with my mom and slapping her on her legs. I was calling her fat and pinching her thighs. She then hit me in the stomach—right where my navel ring is. I screamed out loud and ran into the living room and threw myself onto the couch.

My mom laughed and said, "You need to quit lying because I didn't even hit you that hard."

"If only you knew," I said to myself. "If only you knew."

It's been almost four months now since I've had my piercing. Four months of agony and caution. Having to be careful about how I sleep at night. How I hug people. How I put on and take off my clothing.

My piercing's like a pet. I have to care for it every day and be more mindful of what I do.

When it hurts, I feel like I want to remove it. Even though I clean it twice a day, it's still sore and irritated half the time. But I know that when it finally heals, I'll be glad that I kept it in.

Symbol of My Independence

My parents still don't know about my piercing. I make sure to hide it well. I hope they don't find out anytime soon because I know I'll be done for. I can imagine them ripping it out of my stomach and stepping on it.

I'll probably tell them on my 18th birthday. Then I'll legally be an adult and they may be upset, but there'll be nothing they can do about it.

Sometimes I feel bad that I disobeyed my parents, but they can't make decisions for me forever. I think they need to realize I'm growing up.

I don't regret my piercing—it hurts a little but it shines. When I look down and see the ring, I see a symbol of my individualism and independence.

Reconnecting with a Rich Heritage Through Body Art

Manu Neho

Having grown up in ignorance of her Maori ancestors and with people rejecting her Maori heritage, the author reclaims her culture and receives a traditional facial tattoo, a moko, *a sign to her and everyone that she is proud of who she is. Manu Neho lives in New Zealand.*

I was born in the Bay of Islands [New Zealand], up north. I grew up with my grandparents, my mother and father, and was the oldest grandchild of all the grandchildren on my father's side. We lived up north until I was nine, and then we moved to Auckland.

I don't have this conscious memory, but I believe my mother told me that when I was three weeks old, my grandfather took me into the forest, into what we call the *nahiri*. And he took me there for a week. And there in the *nahiri*, I believe I was given lots of information of how we are, why we are, and how we will be. So that was on a spiritual plane.

My grandfather died in 1958. And at that point, I was four years old. Now, in my mind, everything stopped. The death of my grandfather had such a traumatic effect on me that I stopped speaking Maori, which was my first language. My first recollection of having anything to do with the European population was when we moved to Auckland and I started school at Richmond Grade School. . . And I didn't realize that I was actually Maori, I suppose if you like, until a teacher called me [a derogatory name]. And that wasn't devastating, you know, because I had shut everything out. From the death of my grandfather, I'd shut everything out, I'd turned off my Maori, it was so traumatic.

Rediscovery of Her Maori Heritage

And from then on, right up until I was about thirty, I believed that [Maori struggles] were valid, but I also thought that people should do things, you know, get up and do things rather than protest about it. I had some real colonized views about how things should happen. And being part of a religion and growing up as Mormon didn't assist the process. So you were a Mormon and you weren't a Maori. And—rightly or wrongly—that's how I felt right up until I was thirty. It was hard for my family when I became a Maori again. It was really hard for them.

The Decision to Get a *Moko*

I think that subconsciously I've always wanted to have a *moko* [permanent body and facial marking]. I suppose it has a lot to do with that week in the bush at three weeks old. There are some things you know instinctively and there are some things that you learn. You have an accumulation of inherent knowledge and learned knowledge. And so I believe the *moko* is part of my inherent knowledge. Having left the Mormon Church and having made that decision to be more Maori, to take up an active political struggle of the way that we were, it just was a natural progression to physically stumble upon *ta moko*.

Then you know it's only natural that one should have a yearning. And having awakened that yearning, it became a need to actually move it from a yearning to a reality. So we had a huge day—a weekend, in fact, here where four women took the *moko kawai* and several others had pieces of work done on them, on their bodies. Our children all had pieces done that weekend.

I had made the decision on a Saturday morning and called my mother. When I talked about my *moko*, she said, "Oh, no,

Manu. If God wanted you to have that, you would have been born with it." And I said to her, "Well, if God wanted you to have clothes, you would have been born with that as well." To which she replied, "Don't be stupid," to me. [LAUGHS] So that was a lot of fun. . . . However, she wasn't pleased about it and we didn't speak again until after I had come back from Samoa. But her whole thing is that she's so devoted to the church and its beliefs that anything outside of that square is not the norm for her.

So having made that decision to have my *moko* was a real big decision. It needed to be swift so that it would happen and it would be over, and then I would have it. And it was really done not only for myself, but I did this for my grandchildren and my children.

The Ceremony and Rebirth

[I had my *moko* done with] three other women. It was a lovely weekend in October 1999. It was important that I have it done before the millennium, before the year 2000. It was also important that it was done in a place where I had some control. It was important that I had the people that mattered the most around me, and that there were some control mechanisms in place in terms of who, how, why, and what for. So we had it here.

[First we had] a *wamea*—a time where we explain and learn about the history of *ta moko*, the process that will happen, and what is expected of those who come. So we had seventy people here. The majority were my family and very dear friends who came to support. And it was a time of celebration, because it was a revitalizing in our particular family of this art form which had almost died and has been revived, so it was a big celebration.

So the highs and the lows were just absolutely wonderful. And people sobbed their hearts out, and it was a huge cleansing of souls and cleansing of spirits, and cleansing of history.

It was absolutely wonderful. I think it was my rebirthing. Because as I sat up after I had been completed, there was this overwhelming sense of rebirth. Just I sat up and the tears just flowed. I sobbed, literally sobbed, as I held onto each one of those that were here to support. I just cried and we held each other, and we have photos of all of that. It was a busy time . . .[with a] spiritual language that no words of this plane can ever describe.

Moko Kaiwai Design

The design of my particular *moko kaiwai* is significant to my genealogy, my *whaka papa*. And incorporated in that *whaka papa* is a shark that's swimming from the Pacific to Aotearoa [Maori name for New Zealand], which symbolizes my mother coming to New Zealand, meeting my father, and then I'm the result. And the rest of it talks about where I was born, which means two rivers. And so it's significant that there's a lot of water flowing. The particular *hapu* or subtribe that I belong to is *Teorewai*, which means "to gently swivel the water so that it ripples and splashes just a little." And then of course, I live on the edge of a lake. . . . And so water figures a whole lot in this particular design. And it's a design that links me with my roots of origin and it keeps me in line.

Also . . . there seems to be either a V or an N, which I might add, adds character to my *moko*. The line is supposed to be a straight line that goes from one side to here. But as my cousin was stretching and [the artist] was working, my oldest granddaughter was so consumed with the fact that they were hurting me that she leaned forward, bumped my cousin, who bumped my chin, who bumped the artist, and there was a little notch in there. [One of the people present] looked at [the artist] and he said in a glance and a little bit of a raised eyebrow, I'll fix it up on the other side. And so there is a real neat character thing to my *moko*.

The whole idea of the *moko* has been a wonderful idea. It is a wonderful reality. I find it the most wonderful fashion addition. It's a wonderful accessory. It looks wonderful in the garden as it does dressed up with diamonds and pearls. But it looks wonderful just with an old hat and a gardening shirt and a trowel as I'm in the garden tending to the roses. So it's at home anywhere, and I'm at home anywhere with it. And it's just natural. Our grandchildren love it.

Public Reaction to the *Moko*

Oh, for the first year, it was a novelty. For the first six months, people would leap out in front of you and stare or sort of stalk you in a shopping mall. And invariably, they were white people, *paki* people. And they were always positive comments. Always positive comments. The negative comments have come from our own people. They're not so negative as lack of understanding statements, I think: "Why did you do that to your beautiful face?" I think that they just don't have an understanding for themselves.

Nonnatives and *Moko*

The reality [of *moko*] is that it has a specific cultural purpose. And whilst it's to adorn the body, and it's for the beautification of the body as seen by the wearer, I suppose, I must say that I was absolutely shocked when I got off the plane in Samoa in 1999, and Gordon and I went out into the airport terminal after collecting our luggage and there was a woman with a *moko*. I think I was noncommittal about how I felt about this. It didn't enrage me, but as the time went on during the convention in Samoa, I think I became a little miffed that it was seen as a *moko*. And I sought to address that with this particular person. And she was really gracious. I think we were both gracious when we talked about it, and she said she hadn't intended it for it to be a *moko*, that she had dreamt and dreamt and dreamt and dreamt, and it just kept coming, this particular design kept coming.

And whilst I believe strongly in cultural and intellectual property rights, I see that a person who has felt quite strongly to have this kind of adornment on their person, and in that particular place, is their own choice. Except we can try to preserve our own cultural and intellectual property rights. I think that if one has a respect for a particular culture, and where the art form comes from, and if one acknowledges that that's where it comes from, and goes through channels of seeking the correct logistics of taking on that kind of adornment, I suppose [it's alright]. [To not acknowledge its origin] I would see as an affront to that particular culture. . . And I do feel affronted when people just blatantly disregard process. And there are processes. So that's my feeling on that.

A Tattoo Tells a Person's Life Story

Tina Firesheets

Inspired by her husband's having her Korean name tattooed onto his wrist, the author discovers that she wants to connect with the different cultures, histories, and families she is a part of, through body art. She retells the painful yet joyous process and writes about the meanings of her tattoos. Tina Firesheets is a staff writer for the News & Record *in Greensboro, North Carolina.*

I've been told that I don't seem like the type of person who would get a tattoo.

I work in an office and am, by nature, fairly conservative. Until recently, I never gave tattoos much thought.

I just couldn't think of anything I wanted on my body permanently. One of my friends has Tigger on her thigh. Tribal tattoos are popular, as are fairies and butterflies. A lot of young women like to get tattoos on their lower back, where they're visible over low-rise jeans.

None of these appealed to me.

A Change of Heart

Then in January, my husband got my Korean name, Lee Sang In, tattooed in English on the inside of his left wrist. The script is so beautiful and elegant. And I love the sentiment behind such an act.

So I began to think about getting one, too. And the more I thought about it, the more confident I became of what I wanted.

My tattoo tells the story of who I am, and what matters to me—my family.

The dogwood blossom above my wrist reminds me of my grandmother.

We used to read together. We'd sit for hours on opposite ends of the same couch and immerse ourselves in Zane Grey and Jane Austen novels.

My grandmother loved dogwoods. She wore a silver necklace with a dogwood blossom pendant.

I have to lift my arm to see the pink cherry blossom just above the inside of my wrist. It reminds me of my adoptive mother who was Japanese. Although she lived in the United States more than 30 years, she never got her citizenship. She missed Japan.

The Korean characters between the dogwood and cherry blossoms represent Lee Sang In, the name I was given before my parents adopted me. Above that, in beautiful script, is my married name: Firesheets. For me, it's more than my husband's last name. It also belongs to his parents, two of the finest people I've ever known.

The "F" curls to form the outline of a cherry blossom petal. The "T" and last "S" curve to outline the dogwood petals.

The Pain of Getting Tattoed

People asked if it hurt.

When I was a kid, I slid on a patch of wet grass and scraped my elbow on some rough gravel. That's what getting a tattoo felt like—scraping yourself on gravel. For about an hour.

It's uncomfortable, but not unbearable. My husband played his guitar to distract me.

The tattoo gun buzzed like a small drill. Chris was my tattoo artist. His breath was warm on my arm.

I thought about a woman I interviewed once. Her name was Betty and she always wanted a tattoo of Betty Boop. So when she turned 80, her son took her to get one. They went out for margaritas afterward.

If 80-year-old Betty could get through it, then I certainly could, too.

In Japan, tattoos were initially used to mark criminals. But in time, it became an aesthetic art. Since only the upper class could wear ornate clothing, the middle class began to get elaborate full-body tattoos.

Tattoos Are Becoming Acceptable

Here in the U.S., people with tattoos were once considered strange and even traveled the freak show circuit. Then it became something that was associated with criminals, sailors or gang members.

Although some employers still believe that tattoos give an unprofessional appearance, it's becoming more mainstream. Some people get portraits of loved ones or their family names tattooed on their skin. Religious portraits or symbols also are popular. Your average housewife or teacher gets a tattoo now.

My husband got his first tattoos about 30 years ago, long before they became socially acceptable. He warned me that having a tattoo, especially one that was visible, might change people's perception of me.

Perhaps it will. But the more you know who you are, and what matters to you, the less it bothers you.

Tattoo Me Again—And Again

Stephanie Dolgoff

In this selection, writer Stephanie Dolgoff explains the complex motivation behind getting her tattoos and finds value in her body art, not only in terms of aesthetics, but also in marking her way to maturity, independence, and fulfillment. Each tattoo becomes the representation of an important development or event and therefore will never fade. Stephanie Dolgoff is the health director of Self *magazine.*

Anyone who tells you that getting a tattoo doesn't hurt is either lying or lying. Or she may be so hopped up on Vicodin that although the process is torturous, she's too loopy to care. Or it might be like childbirth amnesia: She's so pleased with the results that she's blocked out what it feels like to have an electric needle scraped back and forth over her delicate skin. Any of those would explain why people—like me—get more than one.

I went the Vicodin route when I got my third and most recent tattoo six months ago, popping one pill and then later another, which I had saved from my cesarean section a few years ago. This latest tattoo, two lush pink and plum peonies on my left inner ankle, hurt more than the C-section. (They don't give epidurals for tattoos, after all.) But like I've never regretted having my twin girls, I've never regretted getting my tats or looked back and thought, What was I thinking? That's because I knew exactly what I was thinking all three times.

I got my first tattoo—a small line drawing of one of Picasso's doves—above my right shoulder blade when I was 25, right before I quit my job, packed up my life and moved to Seville to teach English. I'd felt so embraced by the city (and by a guy named Manolo) when I'd visited a few years earlier that I was sure it was my natural home. I didn't wind up staying, but the decision was one of the best I've ever made. I learned that I could fly above life's expectations and rely on myself for all my needs if I had to. (Oh, and that Spanish men who still live with their parents—i.e., most single Spanish men—are a wee bit immature.)

Nine years later, I got a second dove on the small of my back, right before my husband and I became engaged. It signified the calm, soaring feeling I had after years of searching for the right partner. It had partly to do with Paul, who made me feel safe and loved, but even more to do with the fact that I'd grown into a person who knew how to include people like Paul in her life. And the third tattoo, the largest and most painful, those dual-colored peonies situated above my foot? They represent my fraternal twin girls, Sasha and Vivian, two very different flowers growing on the same vine. Now they'll always be with me, even when we're apart.

Each of my three tattoos represents a major emotional milestone or epiphany and serves as a bodily reminder of the freedom I felt because of my new experience or bit of knowledge. They're like signposts along the road to now, someplace I feel lucky to be. When I look at them, I can feel again the exhilaration of the life-altering shift that pointed me squarely toward personal peace and fulfillment. If I'd gotten Denzel Forever on my butt or Hello Kitty on my inner arm during a drunken moment, I might well regret it. In general, though, I'm not a big regretter. I tend to see even the dumbest decisions as learning experiences ("Google? What a stupid name for a company. No way am I investing!"), as opposed to evidence of what a fool I was when I was younger.

My reasons for getting my tattoos make sense to me, and that's all that matters. There are as many reasons to get a tattoo as there are images to express people's personal experiences, memories, emotions or even favorite band, if you feel that strongly about it. The best reasons have this in common: They please the person wearing the body art, not necessarily the person looking at it. One friend got a leafy cuff around her upper arm purely because it made her feel like a hot mama; another went with her best friend and got matching Japanese symbols for happiness, to give their friendship its symbolic due; still another got a C-sized battery on her hip, to remind her that she needs to stop and recharge.

Whatever the meaning, you're more likely to be happy with your tattoo if you have a reason—or reasons, in my case—you can live with forever, like the tattoo itself. You can't think of a permanent piece of skin art as a haircut that, once you're tired of, you can let grow out. And even though it's possible to have a tattoo removed, the process certainly isn't easy. The few people I know who regret their tattoos say they liked them when they got them but now hate what they project to potential bosses or mothers-in-law. It's true that you never know how radically your priorities or career goals (or the names of your lovers—I'm talking to you, Angelina) will change over time. (Case in point: I know a woman who, in her 20s, covered both of her arms in colorful mermaids and ivy vines. She now works with children; the kids think her tattoos are cool, but she wears long-sleeved shirts around the parents, mostly because she doesn't want to lose clients.) But I like to think if I ever forsook writing for, say, holding public office, becoming a trophy wife for a prominent real estate magnate or even turning letters on *Wheel of Fortune*, I'd be so good at what I did that people would forgive my tattoos as one of the eccentricities that come with creative genius. Clearly I'm not that concerned, though—not least of all because I know many hard-driving female CEOs have secret ladybugs, hearts or lotus blossoms hidden under their posh, tailored suits. These days, Satanic pentagrams, swastikas and symbols of anarchy aside, most tattoos hardly signify rebellion.

Although I love my tattoos, I don't plan on getting any more, mostly because I'm running out of spots on my body that will never droop, get stretched out or grow hair—all of which would ruin even the most beautiful, well-thought-out design. After getting the peonies, I told Paul of my decision to call it quits. He said he distinctly remembered my saying that the last time. And he's probably right. So I never say never, except that I know I'll never regret my tattoos.

SOCIAL ISSUES
FIRSTHAND

CHAPTER 2

Health and Social Issues

Tattoos Can Cause Painful and Potentially Dangerous Infections

"Bronzed"

After enjoying her first tattoo experience, the author rushes into a second treatment against the advice of her artist, and soon gets an infection. The infected tattoo lands her in an emergency clinic and not only endangers her health but also the reason for this unwelcome visit: the artwork itself. "Bronzed" lives in Toronto.

Here is my cautionary tale to all of you who will be getting a tattoo in the near future.

Following the success of my first tattoo, I was really riding the wave of the adrenaline high, and decided almost the same day as my first one was done that I wanted a second (and third and fourth, etc.). I returned to [the tattoo parlor] a mere three days later (my first mistake, and I admit this freely) with a design and a mind to be tattooed again.

Wes, my tattoo artist, made it clear to me that he did not recommend having a second tattoo done so soon after the first, as there had been no time for my body to recover. However, having said that, he admitted that it might not be a complete debacle, as the second tattoo was to be only 6 inches away from the first, and my body might accept it as just an extended area to heal. For clarification purposes, my first tattoo is on my left forearm just below the elbow, and the second one is on the top of my left wrist. Under ordinary circumstances, perhaps the healing process would have been normal, but as you will read, this tattoo was not to be anything close to ordinary.

Taking a Risk

Despite his warning I pressed ahead, and he applied the transfer to my wrist. Once we were both happy with the way it was placed, he went ahead and started on the outline. This tattoo was virtually painless, until Wes arrived at the part that covered the area above my wrist bone. This area was quite painful, but bearable. The rest of the tattoo progressed without a hitch, and I returned to work afterward (I had the work done during my lunch break) without many problems.

When I was leaving work, I noticed that the bandage had moved away from the tip of the tattoo, leaving a bit of my fresh ink uncovered a mere 3 hours after application! I began to panic, and used some scotch tape to attempt to stick the bandage back onto my hand, but I believe by this point the damage was done. I returned home, showered, and went to bed not thinking anything else of it.

I awoke early the next morning, a Saturday, to a most unpleasant feeling on my freshly tattooed wrist—my cat was sitting beside me and licking my "wound." Again, complete panic overtook me as I shoved the cat away and ran to clean the tattoo again, but no doubt it was way too late to prevent the damage my beloved furry friend had done.

As you can see, my luck with this tattoo was steadily heading downhill, and about to get much worse.

The rest of the weekend progressed without problems, but by Monday afternoon, I was becoming quite worried about my tattoo, as it had developed a lot of redness in the area which my cat had been licking. I tried to ignore it, but bit the bullet on Tuesday after work and headed over to [the tattoo parlor] for Wes to give it the once over.

I dont think I will ever forget the look on his face when he saw that tattoo. I must admit, I never thought I would see a tattooist blanch, but pale he did! He advised me to put creme polysporin on it (and I must note here that polysporin is only recommended by Wes in cases like mine, the beginnings of an infection), and to see the doctor if it continued to get worse.

A Trip to the Emergency Room

I began using the polysporin three times per day, as instructed, but despite my efforts the tattoo only continued to get worse. By Friday, one full week after the tattoo was done, things were really in dire straits. I had an appointment with Wes to plan my third tattoo (which is now in progress), and he insisted on having another look at the problem child. I told him I already had a doctor appointment the next day for it, but after seeing it, he told me I had better head over to an emergency clinic [that day], as even another 24 hours would be far too long to wait.

So, off to the doctor I went that night, somehow managing to avoid any kind of lecture from the emergency clinic doctor before he prescribed me some antibiotics, he even went so far as to say it was a "damn good thing" I came in when I did, as more than another two days or so of waiting would probably have landed me in the hospital.

Long story short, I was on the antibiotics for ten days, and it wasn't until the end of the ten days that my infection really showed signs of improvement. The entire area around the infection was very red and swollen, and extremely tender. Pain would shoot all the way up my arm if the area brushed even against my clothes.

Thankfully, I had a remarkable recovery, and did not lose much of the ink in my tattoo. Wes had me come in so he could see how it was doing, and exclaimed that he had expected me to lose most of the ink, as the infection could potentially have travelled through the whole tattoo.

A Learning Experience

I have learned a lot from this experience. If you are uncomfortable with the bandaging job that is done to your tattoo, or think an area might be left vulnerable to the gauze slipping off, PLEASE say something to your artist! They are more than happy to add more gauze and tape it down more, you need only ask! If you must be at work with a fresh tattoo, make sure you are paying attention to it, and keep things from hitting on it. Keep your pets out of the room for the first few days, as they will see your tattoo as a wound, and want to lick it better (my dogs have all tried to do this for each tattoo I have had done).

Above all other advice I have from this experience, if you notice that one area of your tattoo is red, hot to the touch, the redness is spreading out from the tattooed skin, and it is more painful to the touch than the rest of your tattoo, PLEASE see your artist! And if it continues to get worse, do not wait as long as I did to see the doctor. . . .

I hope that someone will read this experience and learn from it, because I know I certainly did, and before this happened to me I didn't know that tattoos could even become infected to start with.

A Tongue Piercing Ends in Oral Surgery

Christina Howorun

To hide a sizeable tongue piercing from the critical eyes of her father, the writer places it so far back that after a few years she develops gum loss and jaw pain. After putting off medical procedures, the infection spreads and threatens her bones, making oral surgery necessary. Christina Howorun is a journalism student at Ryerson University in Toronto.

"It'll feel like a pinch," the tall muscular man with the shaved head and tattooed neck reassured as he washed his hands in a stainless steel sink.

His clamp-meets-single hole punch tool reflected the beads and rings that hung from his lips, eyebrows and nose.

I nervously opened my mouth, stuck out my tongue and said, "Ah."

He was right. It felt like my tongue had somehow run into my little sister's malicious fingers. Within minutes it was just a small sting and my swelling tongue sported a silver, 14-gauge tongue ring.

The pain came nearly five years later.

Like many of my Generation Y cohorts, I fell victim to the trend of self-mutilation. At 16, I got my first non-traditional piercing, a belly-button ring. I remember my friend tagging along, holding my hand and cringing when the piercing specialist stuck the gun through my skin. I was hooked.

That summer, I got a tattoo just above my right hip: a small, meaningless pink heart with a purple daisy breaking through.

The next summer, I added another: the Japanese symbol for princess on my lower back. I took a break, and it wasn't until I hit 21 that I entered the world of tongue jewellery.

Piercing My Tongue

Fearing my father's wrath, I was careful to get the stud about 3 cm away from the tip of my tongue. I was certain he couldn't see it there, and if he ever did, he never said anything about it.

For safe measure, I got a rubber backing for the bottom of the stub. The tattooed man at the piercing shop assured me that this would prevent any damage to my gums. I was content, and stayed that way for over four years.

Then, last December, what should have been an uneventful trip to the dentist ended up costing my insurance company $1,400, and me 10 days of anguish. When I opened my mouth, the hygienist was appalled. I had "considerable" gum loss behind one of my teeth; she pegged it at 3–4 mm. The tooth had "mobility" and could eventually fall out, she cautioned. She urged me to remove the stud and visit a periodontist, a gum specialist.

Reluctantly, I removed my mouth jewellery and saw the doctor.

If the hygienist was appalled, the specialist was shocked. The lanky man with thick glasses and a kind smile immediately ordered a tooth-and-gum X-ray. "Are you sure you haven't been experiencing severe pain in your jaw?" he asked, actually using the word 'severe.'

No, I was fine. In disbelief, he reached for the X-rays and pointed at fuzzy white-and-black spots. The doctor pulled out a model of a mouth, and peeled away its rubber gums to reveal teeth roots and bones. My gum loss, he said, was the least of my problems. An infection was spreading across my jaw line, eating away at my bone and teeth.

I was going to need surgery and fast. He would remove my gums, clean out the infection and give me several injections of fetal pig teeth protein. Hopefully, he said while pointing to the bone loss on the X-ray, he could rid my mouth from disease and encourage new growth.

Hopefully?! He wasn't certain he could get rid of the infection? He hoped this pig stuff would make my bones grow?! He wanted $1,400 and he wasn't positive this would work. Visions of developing a snout and curly tail danced in my head.

I would need at least seven days to recover. I protested. I couldn't take that type of time off school. I booked my appointment for late April. It was only two months away, I reassured myself. How bad could it get?

From Bad to Worse

It was just before St. Patrick's Day when the severe pain took over. My mouth was in anguish. Sharp, fiery pangs shot up my jaw line. I was in constant pain.

I developed a routine. Tylenol 3's at night and Advil Extra-Strength all day let me get through my classes for just over a week. But it was getting worse.

My doctor saw the mess that was quickly taking over my mouth. The infection was spreading, eating at my jaw; I needed surgery now.

The procedure was fuzzy. I was drugged and frozen, but I'm certain I felt every scrape against my jaw bone. I left with a mouth full of thick black stitches, throbbing gums and a bag of drugs.

The next week was an OxyContin-induced haze. Frozen bags of spinach defrosted on my cheeks. Mountains of pills were ingested each day, applesauce became an entrée and sleeping for 16 hours of 24 was the norm.

Facing the Consequences

I won't know if the pig protein worked for some time. But the infection that was tearing away at my bones is gone.

I'm no longer in pain and the stitches are gone, although I still can't use my front teeth or enjoy a sandwich.

My situation wasn't unique. Dr. Wayne Karp, a Toronto-area periodontist, says that tongue rings can result in gum and tooth damage. Most often, "it's gum recession, but it depends on where the stud is, how your tongue hits your gums and how big the piercing is," he says.

Gum grafts, where a periodontist removes part of a mouth's roof and transplants the gum to the affected area, are much more common. My situation, "doesn't happen frequently, but as you know, it does happen," Karp says.

It turns out that being trendy can be destructive.

More than 500 bacteria call your mouth home and with more openings for these germs to explore, serious bacterial infections can destroy the supporting bones that hold your teeth in place.

"Contact with the jewellery can cause teeth to crack or chip and your gums to recede," says Ontario Dental Association spokesperson Dr. Janet Tamo. "Once you start peeling away at your gums, it (the piercing) starts hitting at the bones and teeth. Losing a tooth is a lot easier than you think."

I look at women on the subway with fried hair from all the perms, crimping and teasing that was popular in the 1980s, and wonder if there are always negative consequences to trends.

Then I eye my meaningless heart/daisy tattoo. Anyone know a good removal specialist?

Tattoo Removal Is a Long and Painful Process

Anonymous

After almost twenty years and many comments on his snake tat-too, the writer has enough of his foray into body art and seeks help at a laser removal studio. He pays the price for his adoles-cent decision to get tattooed with pain, frustration, and, finally, hope that at the end of the long process the snake will have faded away.

Wow, a snake. Why you might ask, would I get a snake tattooed on my forearm in the first place? I do not have the faintest idea why I did it. Oh yes now I remember. It was 1989 and I was 17. Metallica, Motley Crue, and Guns and Roses owned the airwaves. I drove a 1973 Mach 1 Mustang and I wanted a Shelby GT 500 in the worst way. So I thought I would get the tattoo now and the car later. (The Shelby co-bra actually faces the other direction, but hey, what the hell do you want from me? I was 17 which made me borderline retarded, not to mention I thought Kurt Russell was cool in *Escape from New York*). Things were great, got the tattoo, but time moved on.

About three years later I realized that I was getting older and maybe having a huge snake tattooed on my arm was a bad idea. People either

1. Thought I was a criminal

2. Thought I put on a "lick and stick" tattoo

3. Asked me, "Do you still like it?" In other words, "It looks like ass."

Anonymous, *Laser Tattoo Removal*. www.piggysmacks.com. Reproduced by permis-sion.

4. Actually gave me a compliment—(usually other people with visible tattoos)

5. Mocked it mercilessly. . .

Time for Action

I am now 35 years old, married, and have a 1-year-old child. I have been a professional programmer for over ten years and the benefit of having a tattoo in an office environment is hard to find. Interviews for new jobs and with clients were always done with a long-sleeved shirt. After having the tattoo for 17 years, its time has come.

Being proficient with the internet, I set out on a search to see what laser tattoo removal was all about. I found a lot of web sites describing the technical details of the lasers and the risks involved, but I never saw any before-and-after pictures of actual removals. I was wondering why they were not proudly displaying the results to get more people interested in tattoo removal. I even had an appointment at a laser clinic once and when I asked the doctor for before-and-after pictures, he got very defensive and said everyone is unique and that showing me before-and-after pictures would not do any good. I thought it was very weird and had a bad feeling about it. I left without making an appointment.

Three years later I finally made an appointment at [a tattoo removal studio] and had the first treatment done on March 6, 2007. . . . The treatments are every 6 weeks, so this is going to take a while. The removal is being performed by an Nd:YAG Q-switched laser by a doctor. The actual laser equipment is called a Medlite C6.

The First Treatment

I showed up for the appointment not knowing what to expect. All I knew is that I was finally getting rid of my god-awful tattoo. I was told about the laser equipment and that there was a chance of scarring and partial skin discoloration. I was told not to proceed unless I totally hated the tattoo. Needless to say I didn't want my tattoo to reach legal drinking age, so I decided to continue.

The doctor took the laser and showed me that on normal skin the laser had no effect. They use different wavelengths for the different ink colors. Hitting white skin had zero impact. She asked me if I wanted freezing and I declined, since the whole procedure would only take 20 seconds.

Right before she started she said, "This is really going to hurt!"

Snap, snap, snap.

Me: JESUS CHRIST!!!!!!

Doctor: Would you like me to stop or continue?

Me: JUST GET IT OVER WITH!!!!!!

I read somewhere that getting a tattoo removed with a laser feels like bacon grease splatter. I would tend to agree with that statement if the grease was molten lead. I would like to say that I have a pretty high tolerance for pain, but this felt like a red hot needle piercing my skin a thousand times a second being dragged across my arm. It was probably one of the longest twenty seconds of my life.

After the treatment was over, it felt like a third degree burn for about 3 hours. . . .

The Second Treatment

I showed up for my second treatment fully knowing what to expect. I was told that this time would not hurt as much as the last time, which I didn't believe. I put on the safety goggles and he started.

Not as much snapping this time. . . . no swearing. . . . much better.

It has lightened up quite a bit and is progressing better than I ever thought possible. . . . I required no bandages or ointment. I was pretty puffy after the appointment, but . . . it only feels like a bad sunburn now. I forgot to mention . . .

that the procedure smells. You would think that it would smell like burnt flesh, but it doesn't. It smells like burning ink (which reeks bad!). . . .

The Third Treatment

I showed up for my third treatment. Being a pro at it now, I was pretty confident going in. For the first time I saw other people coming out from their appointments. They take pictures before every treatment and the secretary was showing one of the patients the progression of their removal. Their tattoo was also black and after four treatments the tattoo was nowhere near as light as mine. The secretary explained that different people react differently at different rates because of their immune systems. There are also other factors such as depth of the tattoo, ink used, and age of the tattoo.

The doctor had a student doctor perform this session while he watched. Same time as last; it hurt nowhere near as bad as the first treatment. It did hurt enough to have me squirming in my seat. . . .

Again, I have to say I am impressed with the clinic and the results so far. The doctor seemed impressed with how much the tattoo has lightened as well. He is shortening the time between appointments from six weeks to four weeks.

The Fourth Treatment

This appointment went like all the others. I sat down, put on the goggles, and he went to work. First on the red ink, then purple and then the black and yellow. Each color requires a change in the laser wavelength. The doctor is really impressed with the progress so far, he has also stated that it may take 7–8 treatments to completely remove the tattoo. . . . After every treatment, the black fades just a touch more. . . . The pain during the treatment was tolerable, only a little bit of snapping. . . .

It is kind of disappointing. I thought that I would be seeing almost total removal by now. I am seeing progress and I know that it will eventually be gone. Hopefully by Christmas at least. . . .

Just the other day I had a stranger ask me if I was getting "laser done." I was happy that someone that doesn't know I am having my tattoo removed noticed that it is disappearing.

The Fifth Treatment

This treatment was a good one. . . .

Wow has this one ever blistered!!!! There wasn't much pain but this is the worst blistering I have ever had. I think the power was bumped up because the tattoo is getting so light. When I look at it in the light at home, it looks a lot lighter . . . you can see lines disappearing that were once there. . . .

The Sixth Treatment

Finally had my sixth session today and it was one of the more interesting sessions so far. They had a television crew on site taping my removal session and the removal sessions of two other people. I was interviewed and asked about when and why I got the tattoo and why I was getting it removed. I even got to mention [my] website. Whether my interview will be aired or not I will just have to wait and see. . . .

With camera rolling she started. I think she took it easy on me this time, the last one was rough and took a while to heal. Again, this is not hurting anywhere near what the first session did. . . .

It is looking much lighter now. However, I can see that the yellow is going to be problematic. I knew this going in, so if you are planning on getting a tattoo, avoid yellow.

The Seventh Treatment

This appointement was a quick one. Nothing out of the ordinary to report. It still hurt a little bit but was very tolerable. There were no blisters this time.

I thought that by now I would be seeing dramatic results. . . . It seems I have reached a plateau with the fading. I keep getting asked how many more treatments it's going to take, and I honestly don't know the answer. Guess I will have to wait and see. Hopefully I will be snake free for summer of 2008.

Why I Rue My Tattoo

Cynthia Searight

The writer recounts her story of getting tattooed for a second time without taking the time to find a satisfying design. Years later she still regrets her lower-back tattoo and her rush into body art. Yet she also accepts that her tattoos are part of who she was and who she has become. Cynthia Searight is creative director of Self *magazine.*

I got my second tattoo when I was 19. For two hours, I lay belly down, butt up, with my Levi's pulled low enough to have a good plumber look happening. Doc, the tatted-out, 50-something shop owner, hunched over my bum, his wiry gray hair dusting my skin and his buzzing, needled handpiece imprinting me with what turned out to be a permanent Rorschach inkblot. Not exactly the swirling design I initially had in mind. I wanted an image that was one part delicate, one part strong, like something you'd see on a fancy wrought-iron gate. Instead I was branded with an abstract, somewhat vulgar design with a point directed straight down my crack.

"Wow, it's great," I said, lying through my teeth, still gritted from the needle's sting.

"Hot. Really hot," Doc said. My friend Jessie, seated next to me and there for moral support, offered similar affirmations. But a little voice inside of my head said, Ugh.

It wasn't Doc's fault. He was a pro; I was the amateur, an amateur at thinking things through. I had thought I possessed that skill. It had been present a year earlier when, in the same chair, with Jessie by my side, I got my first tattoo, a good-luck ladybug southwest of my belly button.

Jessie and I got our first tats together to spice up our senior year at Catholic school. Three times before the appointment, I drove my 1988 Oldsmobile to the library, where I sat cross-legged in my uniform kilt, thumbing through books, looking for the perfect depiction. The spot I had chosen on my body was a bit clichéd but easily hidden from potential employers and by a wedding dress. (That was my mother's sole wish, which I granted because she was less than thrilled about the tattoo but didn't try to stop me.) When it was done, I loved it. I loved it even after someone pointed out that, thanks to the ladybug's tilt and placement, it looked as if a bug were crawling out of my underwear.

But when I got that second tattoo a year later, there was no research involved. I simply made a decision right before the lower-back-tattoo trend took off. To me, the tattoos, and those who sported them at the time, seemed tough—in a good way. If I got one, I thought, I would still be a nice girl, the occasional Ann Taylor shopper and A student, but I'd be drawing out the Sonic Youth–listening, beer-swigging badass I also identified with.

I gave Doc the picture of the design, which I had found on a friend's T-shirt. He said it wouldn't reproduce with the same detail on my skin but that he'd sketch something similar that would. My critical mistakes came after that: The final design wasn't exactly what I wanted, but I convinced myself that it looked cool enough (mistake one). Not only was I too shy to ask for other sketches (two), but I was so eager to get the tattoo that I spent 30 seconds thinking it over after seeing the drawing (three). Once I saw the stencil on my skin, I thought, it will be fine. The Ugh voice was there, but I ignored it. Perhaps the voice, likely dressed in a cashmere sweater set, was being smothered by a badass in a concert tee.

In the weeks after, I lied to friends about my feelings. I even tried to convince myself that I liked the tattoo, that it conveyed the tough side I was desperate to show off to the world in order to balance my good-girl side. A few months later, though, I started seeing girls everywhere (and not only the tough types that had initially inspired me) sporting lower-back tattoos. Mall rats in belly shirts, cheerleaders, sex sirens, moody emo-girls and preppy blondes all showed off ink when bending over to pick up their pom-poms/mix tapes/polo mallets. I had little in common with these girls before my tattoo, but now we were officially connected. My plan had backfired. Not only might people get the wrong idea about me, they might actually get the worst idea: that I was yet another too-trendy girl who thought tattoos were just, like, so cool. I might as well have asked for a tattoo that said "Trying too hard."

Acceptance, Eventually

Somewhere along the way, though, the regret started to fade. At first it was superficial realizations: I thought, At least I didn't get an ex-boyfriend's name or a Chinese character that instead of meaning beautiful symbolizes harlot. But then, as I graduated from college and began living on my own and flourishing in my career, I started to feel more comfortable with myself at a deeper level. I liked the person I had become and accepted all the decisions I had made along the way, including the tattoo. While at a friend's wedding, reflecting on how marriage would change her life, I began to ponder my own path and realized that I had, in fact, become a real badass. To me, that had nothing to do with listening to the right music, wearing the latest clothes or deciding to get my second tattoo—and everything to do with being fearless about my true self and accepting who I was, inside and out.

A decade later, I'm not embarrassed if my tattoo peeks out or friends make a joke. At my grandfather's funeral, for instance, I had to bow at the altar before giving my reading. I was wearing high-waisted pants (thank you, Marc Jacobs, for a rise of more than 8 inches) and a blouse I was certain fell beyond the safety zone. After mass, though, a cousin said, "Father Michael saw your tattoo, and he wanted me to tell you he's very disappointed." He then clapped me on the back and broke into a full belly laugh. I felt good, even honored, that the tattoo could provide joke fodder for my relatives—and that I could laugh, too.

When it comes to regrets, my tattoo falls somewhere between a misguided hookup and the time I drove after one too many beers. For it and all my other mistakes, I've forgiven myself—and instead of contemplating laser removal, I choose to look at the tattoo as a reminder of who I was and who I am now. Sure, I'll keep making mistakes, but I'm smart enough now to recognize and avoid those I may later come to regret. Why spend thousands of dollars erasing this bad decision when I could use the money to make good ones: traveling, helping a friend, buying more Marc Jacobs trousers? And as far as worrying about what people will think of me if they accidentally see my tattoo: If they don't also see that I'm a fun and empathetic friend, a smart woman and a kind and responsible person, then f--- 'em; the badass in me doesn't care.

SOCIAL ISSUES
FIRSTHAND

CHAPTER 3

Piercing and Tattoo Artists at Work

A Notorious Tattoo Artist Discusses His Career

Brandon Bond, interviewed by Chuck B.

Acclaimed tattoo artist Brandon Bond discusses his beginnings and his career in the tattoo industry. While tattoos are works of art, running a tattoo studio is a business, and Bond discusses the two sides of the trade, as well as working with clients and other artists.

Prick Magazine: *Did you see yourself becoming the artist and businessman that you are today back when you started tattooing?*

Brandon Bond: When I started tattooing I was not even aware of the intensity and growth we were all about to experience as an art form, lifestyle, and as a business. The tattoo industry has since gone through a huge rebirth and renaissance and my plans were created on the fly as a result of that growth. Fourteen years ago, there really wasn't anything around like what we are doing today. It was later that 222 Tattoo in Frisco, Darkside Tattoo in Connecticut, Ed Hardy's Tattoo City, and NewSkool Kolectiv in Cali all shaped what people thought about the limitations of the parlor atmosphere. I knew that I was going to do everything in my power to learn and grow and develop my own style, but as I saw artists working together and accomplishing works that consistently blew everyone's minds, I knew that collaboration was the future of tattooing. One artist alone cannot produce art like two or five or ten artists can. Strength is in numbers, but I never forget that it is always quality over quantity. One bad attitude or ego-driven distraction can ruin the mood, and art is all about mood. I worked in 20 cities at a vast number of extremely well-known studios. I had U-Haul on speed dial for over a decade. I moved nomadically seeking better art, better artistic environments, and was consistently disappointed. I knew at some point that I would have to create what I was seeking and set out to make it happen at any cost. I feel extremely grateful to have pulled together the staff and environment that continues to grow here in Atlanta at our studio. I put everything I had into it and fought tooth-and-nail to ensure its success. It was worth it.

Your tattoo studio, All Or Nothing, just celebrated its second anniversary, and it's been one of the most publicized shops in the last few years. Did you have any idea how successful your shop was going to become?

Honestly, we have only achieved about 70 percent of the goals I have in place. But we are still young. I thought it would work, but the level of success we have achieved, and are still achieving, is only the result of hard work with a side dish of luck. My staff and I push each other at every pass; I could not have achieved any of this alone, and I remind them of that as often as possible. As amazing and awesome of a ride as this has been, there is much work still to do. "The only place success comes before work is in the dictionary." That is a quote in my book from my mother, and it's true. We have to remain hungry at all times, motivated and driven.

Your shop name pretty well sums up the type of person you are. You are all or nothing when it comes to art and shop promotion. What have been some of the triumphs and speed bumps that have helped or hindered you in your rise to fame and fortune?

Tattooing is an art form, studio ownership is a business. I think a lot of people blur the line between the two. I refuse to let my staff starve. The only purpose in business is producing revenue and feeding those who depend on it. I feel like a lot of people misunderstood what I was doing early on, and as a result we still have a lot of haters. The "starving artist" mentality that pervades our industry is doing nothing but holding us back. I was simply reaching out to our target demographic as a means to an end. Internet promotion and advertising are key to any successful venture economically. So I hired some people to plaster search-engine-friendly information all over the Internet. Tattoo artists have consistently misunderstood this activity and still do in some instances. If we win a pile of awards and then post it on the Internet we are not being arrogant, cocky, exploitative, or obnoxious; we are simply feeding information to our target demographic: the tattoo client. Why do we need 15 Web sites? Because clients read every single word on all of them and then book a flight to Atlanta. Why have a mailing list? So our clients can be aware of what's going on and which cities we will be appearing in. Why advertise on TV? Why not? Tattooing is no longer a secret, underbelly of negativity. It is a validated art form and a gigantic industry enjoying a level of success that was previously unprecedented. We treated our studio as a business and promoted it. I am not interested in being underground or secretive—this is not the '20s and I see no reason to act like it is. Would I have changed anything? Yes! I probably would have added a disclaimer specifically directed at other tattoo artists saying, "Relax, man. It's cool. This is just for the clients of the universe. Please don't hate the player, hate the game. We are not trying to say we are better than you. We are promoting, so please ignore this unless you want to get a really dope tattoo." . . .

What's the best way to describe your new book, "Whore,"
and why was it something that you wanted to put together?

I was approached about doing a book two years ago. A company asked me to send them some drawings and photos, and then they would do the rest. I blew them off, knowing that anything I put together would have to be completely controlled by my graphics team and uncensored. Their offer inspired me and I began a journey to create something extremely personal, powerful, motivating, artistic, and f---ed up. It took us two years of working every day on it. Every page is a piece of art, an uncomfortable window into an extremely disturbing and blunt reality. I address every aspect of tattooing, sexuality, relationships, promotion, exposure, motivation, money, frustration, being a boss, hatred, love, despair, and success. I touched on every subject that we could force into the 170-plus pages. There is text, photos, drawings, blood splatter, firearms, nudity, money, short stories, and deeply personal messages exploding throughout the book. It's pretty insane and every word is completely honest in every way. In fact, it's too honest at times.

You recently announced your retirement. Are we still going to see new Brandon Bond tattoos?

Yes, I am still tattooing. The honest truth is that I couldn't handle the amount of clients flooding my appointment book. We have booked the rest of the year, and we aren't taking many new clients. I am not all art fagged out, or trying to dissuade any potential clients, however I'm dying from way too many hours of tattooing. I worked seven days a week for over a decade, literally. This is actually a large part of what my book is about. I haven't done anything but tattoo since I was 17 years old, and I need room to breathe. Still, I don't know anything other than tattooing. It is my life. I'm not abandoning it, just backing up off of it. I will no longer be tattooing at conventions, doing guest spots, no more crazy tour schedules, and hopefully things will not be so hectic in my everyday life. I will still be teaching in convention seminars, but not trying to tattoo my ass off.

Tell me about your new studio, A.N.T.I. Art Elite.

I wanted to be able to tattoo in an environment that I could not be distracted in, an area where we could do collaborations without interruption. This studio I have built is incredible, complete with movie theaters, koi fishponds, huge drawing areas, an art gallery featuring my own private collection of works from all over, and the most laid-back, luxurious setting imaginable. Clients cannot get tattooed here without approval. It is not a public studio. It is perfect in every way. It relaxes both the client and the artists to the point of bliss. The days and nights pass as though I weren't even working at times. It made tattooing fun again for me. It's opulent.

When a client comes to you and says, "Do whatever you want," how do you decide what to tattoo on them?

I'm extremely fortunate to have the clients I do. Most of them pick a body part and say, "Fill it up." This freedom allows for an incredible level of consistent experimentation and motivation. I keep a heavy black file folder with me at all times that contains hundreds of sketches, photos, images, disks, and tattoo ideas. I work to overflow this folder constantly. On the day of a client's appointment, I just lay out a few printouts and drawings that fit the body part, and explain what direction I'm pushing toward. From this the client selects the style or imagery he or she is most enthusiastic about. I stay up late into the night regularly, researching, drawing, screwing around with Photoshop, and printing all types of images that intimidate my artistic confidence. I look to do tattoos that are extremely hard to do. Clients really dig going through all the secret files, and sometimes they argue over who gets what, but nothing is wasted. I discuss a lot of this process and how to emulate it in my seminars.

Where has the world of collaborative tattooing taken you artistically in the last year?

Further than I could have ever gone on my own in another 15 careers of workaholism. I learn from every collaboration we do. It is the absolute height of art and growth. The way I look at tattoos is affected by challenging myself to work with another artist who I respect. It's nerve racking, intense, and occasionally uncomfortable, but it creates change, and anyone who fears change in their portfolio is not growing at all. Tattooing with another artist's favorite ink or machines, and using different lighting and colors in the imagery is like a window into another artist's secret creative process with an all-access pass, VIP style. My back piece is a collaborative work, and my new studio is set up specifically for doing collaborations. I cannot explain the magic that happens to your vision by doing this with someone you can be yourself with. My work changes slightly with every artist I work with and I can always see the reciprocal occurrences in the other artists' corresponding portfolios. It's like setting your creative gasoline on fire and drenching it in truckloads of gunpowder. Albie Rock, Dave Tedder, Nate Beavers, Sean Herman, Josh Woods, Lenny Renken, Joe Waulken, and Joshua Carlton have all had an influence on what I do as a result of hours and hours of intensive focused debate while creating mutual works of art together. I will continue to work in this manner regardless. It's so personal and beautiful. It's confident and scary all at the same time. I'm all tingly just thinking about it. You're gonna make me all misty and stuff man. . . .

In becoming who you are as an artist and shop owner, you built a lot of bridges and burned a few. Is there anything that you would do different or take back if you had to do it all over again?

It's weird because I have no regrets, but you can't please everyone. I have been repeatedly misquoted in articles, and people take that stuff so personally. In all honesty I would probably take it personally, too! It's extremely upsetting to everyone involved, especially me! I never meant to intentionally offend or disrespect anyone, but it's bound to happen when you're doing as many interviews per year as I have done in the past five [years]. A couple are going to suck. I am not responsible for what a magazine misrepresents, and I always require a retraction acknowledgment. I hope this is not one of them, as it is very important to me that I not offend other tattoo artists. I have nothing but respect for other artists, especially those who have been in it longer than I. My gratitude is expressed constantly in my work and in print, but that's not the part people seem to notice. It's ironic really, for instance, when you're talking to your old lady and you tell her for five minutes how awesome she is, but all she heard was one sentence in the middle somewhere that offended her. Then, of course, she freaks out and doesn't give you any coochie. I have nothing but respect for tattooing, tattoo artists, and tattoo studios. Without those before us, we would be nothing. People seem to have formulated an opinion about me because of all the crap in these interviews. My book deals with this subject some as well. All I can say is, "Don't believe the hype." If you are offended by my statements, call me, let's talk about it. Don't freak out and talk shit about who I am as a person. I'm easy to find, and a magazine is not a venue in which I would start a war.

You just imported a team of great new artists. Who are these guys and where did you find them?

I honestly could not be more stoked about the talent that just moved in. Dave Tedder and I toured last year all over the country doing conventions, seminars and guest spots. We met hundreds of badass tattoo artists from everywhere, and word traveled that we were looking for some like-minded, driven and talented artists. The first was Nate Beavers from Big Brain in Omaha. He came to our shop to do a few guest spots and just blew everyone's f---ing mind. That guy is on fire. I have already done two collaborations with him, and I have to try to keep up with him. He has been tattooing as long as I have, I think. He's incredible. He can bust out a portrait, a bloody zombie, perfect traditional, and a Japanese sleeve all in the same afternoon without batting an eye. The second was Josh Woodkowski (Josh Woods) from Buffalo, New York. I cannot believe the shit this guy pulls off. He does so many different styles at the same time I don't think he even understands it! Watch out for that guy, he's burning both ends. The third was

Lenny Renken who also comes from Omaha. He is a younger artist who you will soon get tired of being blown away by. We are doing a collaboration piece together in a few weeks. He is growing faster than all of us. These guys with Dave Tedder, Sean Herman, Joe Waulken, a slew of guest artists, and myself combine to form Voltron, and can really destroy some shit. We are always looking to find more hungry and driven talent, and are always hiring. Albie Rock, Justin Weatherholtz, Billy Hill, Dan Henk, and Anthony Orsatti come through regularly and lay the smack down. We are a Leviathan of motivation and creativity, I have to pinch myself to make sure I'm not just hallucinating all of this.

Any final thoughts, future goals or shout outs?

Yes, we have a new addition to the A.N.T.I. family. Dave Tedder is about to reproduce any day now and All Or Nothing has never had a baby! So congrats to Dave and his baby mama. And I'll see all of you in hell.

A Female Tattoo Artist Breaks into a Difficult Profession

"Warlord Kitty"

The author chronicles her early years as a high school dropout and drifter, and her chancing upon a tattoo artist and becoming his apprentice. Through hard work and her devotion to body art, she find a niche of her own and professional fulfillment.

As any apprentice would agree, breaking into the tattoo industry is difficult. It's not something you can go to school for, it is passed down from one generation to another. Tattooing practices are passed regardless of race, creed, color, or religion.

I was 19 years old, I had dropped out of high school on my way out of my small hometown in Indiana. I was sick of my parents, sick of my life and sick of the world. My friend Casey had a car, I had the money. Casey had family in Oxnard, California. That's where we were destined to end up.

We drove for what seemed like days, but finally arrived in Cali, Hollywood to be exact. That was interesting. It was 2 A.M. and people were running, walking, vomiting, being handcuffed, walking on all fours with a dog collar around their neck and being led by a scary-looking women with a leash down the street. Scary shit being 19. I took it more as an experience than fear, even though fear was the first response.

Entering a New World

We made it to Casey's aunt's house, in Oxnard, 4 hours later; we had gotten lost. They were nice people, but I believe they were shocked by my appearance. I was experimenting at the time with hair color, piercings and tattoos, needles with string wrapped around them dipped in ink to be exact. We had something to eat and as I was sitting at the table I couldn't help notice the whispers and stares I was getting. It made me feel uncomfortable and angry. Casey walked up to me at the table and with no emotion told me I had to leave. They didn't care where I went or how I was going to get there. I was too different and had to leave. So I left, threw some choice fingers in the air and proceeded to find a nice warm spot to settle into, behind a dumpster, for hours.

I finally decided I was going to do something; I couldn't live the rest of my life behind a dumpster. Oh and by the way most kids in this situation would have been calling mom or dad collect to wire them money. I loathe my parents.

Nowhere to Go

I ended up walking for hours until I came to the town of Ventura. I hung out for a while on the streets, begging for money to get some food and thought about what the f--- I was going to do. A woman walked up to me and gave me some change and told me maybe I should try going to the welfare department, and I did. They gave me some bus tokens and a coupon for some free food at the local pantry. It helped, but not a whole lot. I stayed on the streets for a while until I eventually got a job at a shit-hole restaurant washing dishes. I saved up my money and got a place of my own, home shitty home. Man this place was a rat-infested, crawling-with-roaches shit hole, but it was a roof over my head and a place to call home. In the process of all this I continued going to the food pantry and developed a great friendship with a man named Steve. He was a nice guy. He had 2 chow puppies in a wagon and every day after we had gone to the pantry we would go to the beach and have a cold, 2-day-old chicken lunch and play with the puppies. I eventually asked him if he would like to come stay with me, since he was also on the streets and I knew how that felt. At first he said no, but I convinced him that friends help each other out any way they can, and that I wanted to help him and his puppies. So he moved in with me, got a job and everything was going just fine in life. He stayed with me for months before I found out he [had been] a tattoo artist from Texas for 23 years.

Building a Future

He had landed a job and I was progressing to less sleazy restaurant work. It was a Friday and we had both been paid. He asked me to come with him somewhere. We hopped on the bus and ended up at a self-storage place. I was kind of perplexed, wasn't sure why we were there, maybe he wanted to get some of his personal stuff out of storage now that he could pay the bill, and needed my help to carry all of it back home. He came out with a huge box and I followed him to behind the storage place under a tree in the grass. He opened [the box] and showed me what would be my life's work.

It was 2 of the most beautiful pieces of machinery known to man or woman, tattoo guns. He had everything, flash, gloves, needles, bars, everything, even ink. It was dried out but he said he could bring it back to life with some Listerine. We took all of these glorious treasures home with us that day and he spent the next year teaching me everything he knew.

The first job I ever worked at was Roy Boy's in wonderful Scary Gary, Indiana. Man that place was frightening for a 20-year-old single chick. They wanted me to sweep the floors, make coffee, feed the big cats and do some stuff I wasn't too thrilled to do. At first Roy Cooper was an asshole to me, real cocky, and acted like he didn't want me there. Then after a while, you could say he grew on me. I spent many a day cleaning the shop and drawing and eventually started tattooing REAL people instead of fruit!

I am now a Female Tattoo Artist with over 10 years experience. I have worked for many tattoo parlors from Indiana to Chicago to New York to Florida. Never in my life before that time did I ever love something with as much passion as I do tattooing, Thank you Steve, wherever you are, from the deepest depths of my soul, thank you.

Making Body Jewelry
for a Living

Pat Pruitt, interviewed by Modified Mind

A jewelry maker discusses how he developed a taste for body jewelry and expanded his love for body art into a business. He also talks about challenges to the industry, such as hygiene and quality regulations, as well as the risks and challenges of jewelry materials. Pat Pruitt is the founder of Custom Steel, a jewelry manufacturer based in New Mexico. His company specializes in designs of surgical steel jewelry.

Modified Mind: *How long have you been making body jewelry?*

Pat Pruitt: I've been making body jewelry for about 10 years now.

Did you start out with Custom Steel or did you start with another manufacturer?

Custom Steel is a Native American original, born and bred in Dallas, Texas, and three years ago moved the company to my home state of New Mexico. For the record, I have not worked with any other company but mine, definitely learned on the fly.

What got you interested in manufacturing jewelry in the first place?

When I was younger, I apprenticed as a traditional silversmith under a local jeweller by the name of Greg Lewis. I found out that I really enjoyed it and to this day still do traditional work for people, but like to keep my traditional jewelry as a hobby. So you could say I had a good grasp of making jewelry when I got into the body jewelry manufacturing biz.

Pat Pruitt, interviewed by *Modified Mind*, "Pat Pruitt: Custom Steel," August 8, 2007. http://modifiedmind.com. Reproduced by permission.

Give us some background on how Custom Steel started. . .

Custom Steel actually started off as a hobby for me in college. I was attending Southern Methodist University in Dallas, Texas, in '91. That is when I personally got involved in the body modification scene. I quickly realized how expensive body jewelry was at the time, and living on a student's budget I couldn't afford much. Keep in mind, at that time 14[-gauge] captive bead rings were selling at about $40–$60 retail.

Having the background and equipment for making jewelry, I realized making the basic ring was no problem at all. I must give [credit] to Allen Falkner of Obscurities Body Piercing in Dallas for helping me out with the right materials for body jewelry. At the same time, I was studying mechanical engineering and got involved in the engineering co-op program at SMU. I had the great opportunity to work in a prototype machine shop for Texas Instruments, where we built components for their LED inspection machines. I was fortunate to study under Geroge Sabolski, a master machinist. He gave me the background in the machining technologies that helped me later on.

So in the beginning, I only made stuff for myself and a handful of friends. I landed a couple of local shops in the Dallas area to sell jewelry to and this provided some extra cash for school. Word got around in the area and I soon had clients in San Antonio, Austin, Corpus Christi, and Houston. I quickly realized that this could actually become a business, so I took the dive, dropped out of school, maxed out the credit cards buying equipment, supplies, etc. . . . and [voila,] I was in business.

From there, we grew slowly, offering just basics. . .captive bead rings, barbells, etc. . . . . It wasn't until '94 that we decided to go into the different styles of jewelry that we made. Starting off with the neo-tribal rings, from there, we just added to the list of products that we now offer. I always tried to make our jewelry extremely practical but unique enough to carry some flair. I don't know if we were the first but definitely one of the first to offer your "nontraditional" designs. Now we have gained the experience to create almost anything, and so we get a lot of requests for custom designs.

Give a quick run-through of the jewelry-making process and the type of equipment Custom Steel uses. . .

The type of equipment that we use varies depending on the particular piece of jewelry that is requested. With your standard items such as barbells, captive bead rings, circular barbells, curved, and basic stuff of that nature, simple tools can accomplish the job. Since we do this at a production level, we have invested in the industrial versions of the [tools].

For the more unique items, we use some industrial belt sanders to carve and grind the appropriate shape of the item. Since each item is hand ground there are slight variances in the product but they still retain their basic shape. The belts that we use are custom made for us, specifically for grinding stainless. We have tried other belts and they tend to wear out quickly and proved to be more of a hassle than anything else. In addition, we have built our own machines or modified others to produce equipment that give us the production capacity that we need. . . .

On the custom items, I pretty much do all the work on those. We have garnered the reputation that if we can't do it, it can't be done. . . .which is pretty cool. So we work with the client, usually via email, to find out what they are looking for exactly. A lot of the time, there are limitations produced by the material itself, or the gauge/ball combination, plus additional factors. So, some of the time what is originally requested may not be possible and we have to work out an alternative solution. Challenging, most of the time, but the client gets something that is practical and is useable.

There are some low-grade jewelry producers out there, do you think there should be regulation on jewelry suppliers to ensure good, safe jewelry, or should it be left up to the suppliers to be responsible?

What can you say about this? Competition is what this country is founded on. There will always be crap manufacturers out there, and what supports them? Price. When a piercer/company is only concerned about price, you will always have people supporting these companies, no matter what the quality is like. On the same note, when the consumer is only concerned about price the support continues.

As for regulation on manufacturers, that's a tough one. In my opinion, if regulation ever occurs it needs to occur at all levels, not just at the manufacturing level. Studios should be regulated, and sellers (nonpiercing) should be regulated as well. For instance, if I were regulated on the materials Custom Steel uses, the manufacturing processes and whatever it takes for us to produce that particular piece of jewerly, would a studio be regulated to purchase that piece from us or another qualified manufacturers? If not, then they could purchase from someone that is not regulated, and probably for a much lower cost. So the regulation would be useless unless it flows down to all aspects of the industry.

Regulation for studios, I think the APP [Association of Professional Piercers] is doing a great job of informing the people that care about what to look for in jewelry manufacturers, but the APP only represents a very small percentage of professionals in the industry. The remaining individuals fall back on the price factor. So regulation at that level, if it ever happens, is going to be a logistical nightmare. You have to imagine that there are thousands of studios that practice piercing in one form or another, not to mention all the piercings that occur in malls around the country. Plus the fact that large corporations have tons of dollars to support them in whatever comes around. I guarantee you if regulation ever hits this industry all the ear-piercing stations in the malls will not be affected. Sad but true, so regulation is a tough question to answer considering all the factors.

On a final note, I believe that all the manufacturers that care self-regulate what they use and how they use them in the manufacturing processes. They strive to bring a high-quality product to market.

What advances do you see in store in the future for the body jewelry industry, and what would you like to see?

As for advances I see three types. The first being material. In England they passed a law that required all jewelry for initial piercing to be made out of a nickel-free stainless alloy.... If that law is carried over to the U.S., you will find almost all the manufactures moving to this 100% nickel free material, Implantanium as it's known. I don't see that happening anytime soon, but you never know.

The second and third are closely related but for different markets. The first being the jewelry manufactured for the postpubescent market for all the little girly girls wanting the next dolphin/teddy bear/strawberry shortcake/glow in the dark/blinking lights/whatever piece for their navel/tongue piercing to impress their little friends at school and raves. I cringe thinking of what is next for them.

The third market is geared for your hard-core piercer/enthusiast that wants really cool but practical jewerly. That's where we come into play. We definitely try to push the envelope with jewelry design but make it a practical piece of jewelry to wear as well. I would also give [credit] to a company called Netherworld. I've seen some of his stuff and it's far out, really cool from a manufacturing point of view, tough shit to make but that's why it's hard to get stuff from him. Another person is Jesse Jarrell, cool titanium plugs/eyelets and such, there's an advancement that is a long time coming. All of his stuff is cast which makes the design process much easier. As for us, we are trying to develop more products for the extremely large-gauge market, when you have a piercing that is ⅝ or larger you have limited options, namely organics, we are trying to develop more products that will cater to them in steel so they have a different option.

What I would like to see, I'll tell you. We are currently working on developing steel items that are similar in design to a lot of organic jewelry that is out there. Unique shapes, carved pieces, and intricated designs out of steel. We are just starting to develop this and it may be another year or or so before we bring this to market. People will flip if we are able to do this, just imagine a ½" spiral out of 316L stainless. . . . ohh . . . my mouth waters just thinking about it.

Body Piercing Is a
Spiritual Experience

Brian Skellie, interviewed by piercing.org

*For the author, piercing was always more than fashion and more
than wearing expensive jewelry in choice parts of the body. In
this interview, he explores the spiritual side of piercing, the an-
cient traditional causes for piercing, and his personal history
that led him to seek a life and career devoted to piercing.*

*A professional body piercer, Brian Skellie discusses the tradi-
tions of his as well as the trend toward better and safer body
piercing within the industry. Skellie owns the Piercing Experience in Atlanta.*

Piercing.org: *How did you receive your training?*

Brian Skellie: My initial experimentation on my own body
came about after inspiration through anthropological sources
such as old encyclopedias, *National Geographic, Smithsonian,*
and reading stacks of dusty old tomes. If nearly every culture
in the world had body decoration before even a written alpha-
bet, it could not be such a complicated thing to do for myself.

If traditional means were sufficient for healing and safety
in a setting other than our urban environment, then I would
need to balance the means to my surroundings so that my immune system would not have to do all of the work itself. I researched the conditions and procedures necessary for successful traditional body adornment of all kinds: *cicatrization*
[healing by the formation of scar tissue], tattoo, ritual burns
such as brands or *moxibustion* [the burning of substances on
the skin to treat diseases or to produce numbness to pain],
body shaping such as corsetry and binding the feet, arms, legs

Brian Skellie, interviewed by *piercing.org*, "A Conversation with Brian," July 11, 2005.
Reproduced by permission.

and head, and the insertion of decorative objects under the skin. I compared all methods I could learn of with scientific and medical research to determine how to emulate these sorts of processes without deleterious effects. Anthropologists' reports of what they saw as 'ruined' body manipulations were often hard to decipher as to indicate infection or trauma. I wanted to carefully avoid any undesirable outcome.

All of this intrigued me at a very early age. The permanent results of the rituals and processes I read about enthralled me, particularly as a personal reminder of experiences. I have collected books and pictures of all sorts of body adornment ever since. I decided to begin altering my own body during adolescence, when I felt my mind and spirit changing at the speed of thought. I put forth a concerted effort to determine what kind of outward mark of my inner growth would feel right to me.

Getting Ready to Self-Pierce

Though the desire for marking my body was apparent to me from early on, I needed much further meditation to find the physical beginning for me. It was not until I was about sixteen and had read and experienced more along the lines of body modification and adornment that I decided I was ready. I chose to put jewelry in my body as milestones of change, a way to remember the wisdom gained from both hard and sweet lessons and experiences.

I put together what I needed to open my skin, and jewelry to put in it. I meticulously cleaned everything as well as I could in a stovetop pressure cooker, chugging away at the highest temperature and pressure it could muster for nearly an hour. I hoped that archaic method would be enough for new unused supplies. I scrubbed my hands and donned latex gloves. I prepared my skin as if for major surgery, with iodine surgical solution in a great big patch around the site. I then changed gloves and set about figuring out how to hold the skin in alignment while putting a sharp piece of stainless steel through my body. About an hour and fifteen minutes later, after numerous changes in my technique, I realized that I simply was not pushing hard enough to break through the skin. The needle was custom made and very sharp stainless steel, but about ⅛th-inch thick, nearly twice the thickness of the ring I intended to put in. This was the major impediment. . . I took a deep breath and bruised my fingers on the blunt end of that shiv in the split second of force it took to go through.

Learning the Trade

I put more thought into the next few pieces that I put into myself and had the next few done by more experienced professionals. I concluded that I should still go about learning more. My closest friends wanted me to put jewelry in for them when they could tell how much it meant to me, and urged me to find a mentor. I met Jack Yount in 1992, a kind and gentle person with over forty years experience, and he steadied my hands and gave them direction. I interacted with as many other experienced individuals as I could to share knowledge and discuss ideas. I observed and was supervised while in Florida, and continued to interact with Jack until he passed away in 1995.

What was involved in your learning process?

I had done enough research in the development of my own techniques, but was not ready to use them on anyone but myself without supervision. I pursued observation of the work of those whom I considered authoritative in the field along with detailed scrutiny of their experiences. I had my hand guided the first few times, and practiced on willing and patient friends under supervision. I continuously work to refine the practical application and broaden my knowledge of the human in change each day.

Learning to work with this change in all of its aspects never stops. The next challenge seems to appear readily and without fail. I tend to eddy off into different ways of seeing the experience to keep it fun and add to the stimulating variety of subtle reactions involved with these shining little things I put in people.

Why and when did you decide to become a body piercer?

I planned to NOT do it for a living, or for trade, just for my friends and myself. When I came back to Atlanta from my first year of college, I made so many appointments within my circle of friends and acquaintances that I rented two rooms with a sink from a retail store, and set about making a studio as Piercing Experience. I met with success and saved my money intending to rent a larger space for exclusively piercing. I spent over a year side tracked, sharing space with a group of tattoo artists, and finally in May of 1995, had found and designed my ideal space. It was a building located one block from where I grew up, and just the right size. I did most of construction myself and had it opened by August. It has been amusing ever since. . . .

What is the most common piercing you perform?

I notice that many of one type of piercing will come to us in a week's time. This I attribute to word-of-mouth promotion by our clients. One good piercing for a happy client can bring in dozens more of the same in time. The common jewelry changes too much to predict. Sometimes it seems obvious, like when someone famous shows off their jewelry, we get many requests for that same sort of thing. I see the media as saturated with that sort of inspiration, just waiting to trigger someone's desires.

What is your favorite piercing to do and why?

A knowledgeable and relaxed client who appears determined to get the best service really brings out the best in me.

I try to talk with people ahead of time until I feel that they are comfortable and informed enough to proceed with a clear conscience.

What kind of sterilization methods do you use?

Sterilization is a clear and simple issue: nothing dangerous should survive the steam sterilization process in our autoclave. I maintain a Statim 2000 cassette sterilizer in proper working condition, test it weekly with bacterial spore samples and an off-site lab to assure that it does kill harmful pathogens, and use it according to its capability.

I researched all available forms of sterilization and determined that a steam would be the best available choice for the implements and jewelry we use. It does not damage our jewelry or leave any dangerous residues. A few novelty pieces cannot be successfully steam sterilized and stay intact, such as acrylic and many plastics, as well as almost all epoxy and glues. We choose not to sell or use any item we can not assure that will be entirely safe based on current scientific standards. We choose not to sell jewelry made with glues and most plastics. Not only do they tend to break too easily, but may conceal and protect pathogens through any sterilization process other than by penetrating radiation. Other types have common disadvantages: heat takes too long and only works for gauze and metal tools; radiation is not available for individual use; and chemical liquid or vapor sterilization have dangerous fumes, may not get all surfaces of objects, and leave dangerous residues.

Is piercing your full-time or part-time job?

Full time since 1992.

What is your perception of body piercing? (Art, fetish, cultural, etc.)

It manifests as a social force, and what I observe depends on the equipment I use. Just as light has wave-like features or particle-like features based on the test and equipment. Today in the microscope it appears as just people who choose to wear jewelry that is harder to lose than a bracelet or necklace; tomorrow with different scopes it may seem mystic, religious, fashionable, fetishistic, an exotic anthropological reflection or a personal symbol. I have dedicated my work to keep it safe, simple, and gentle. Make of it what you will. . . .

Any other information that you could give me about being a professional body piercer would be much appreciated.

I anticipate the eventual decline of anyone practicing non-sterile piercing methods. People are moving towards safer procedures such as wearing sterilized gloves to handle and insert autoclave-sterilized needles, instruments and implant-grade jewelry and steer away from prevalent clean-looking but contaminated procedures. People are beginning to realize that too much has been previously left to guess about in the business, and that there are safer ways to put jewelry in people, without all the loose ends and nagging issues of conscience. I anticipate that clients will choose safer methods based on research instead of perpetuating old guesswork opinions and assumptions.

Caveat vendor; caveat emptor: Seller beware; buyer beware

I am working on refining systems of quality control to provide for public health while still in the best interest of the piercer. It is a challenge to take safety seriously without incurring some expense, whether it be time, labor or cash. It is worth it. . . .

A Female Artist Keeps Tattooing a Family Business

Mendi Klein

Growing up, the author experienced the unique atmosphere of a tattoo parlor firsthand. Following in her father's footsteps, she later learns the trade and becomes herself a successful artist. In this selection, she talks about her motivation and about advancing her art. Mendi Klein lives in Illinois.

Growing up in a small town in Illinois, I had a lot of time to study and watch my father T. "Solo" Haynes. He was and still is my idol. I would sit outside of his office, hearing that tattoo machine just buzzin' away on some lucky customer of the day. When he got going, he did not want to stop. Each time I remember peeking in the door, and he would stop for a moment and smile, wave me over and start telling me about what he was doing. I was in awe! I told him when I was about 8 years old that we were going to have a tattoo shop together.

Well, we now have 2 studios. I wanted to write so people could read about how a small-town girl and her dad go about their lives each day, working with clients we have known forever. Not worried about the world around us, just making our own little dent in the artistic world, and doing it with a humbled smile.

I did my first tattoo over 12 years ago, when I was 18.

I am 31 now and I still learn something new every day. Each client, each work of art, each experience makes me a better tattoo artist. I am also a graphic designer and freelance scratchboard artist. I have been juggling these loves of mine for quite some time. But I would not trade it for the world. The best feeling is when me and my dad are both back in the tattoo studio just working away; we both tend to have the same facial expressions and mannerisms when we tattoo. The clients notice these similarities and just smile.

Making Time for Art

Dreamtime is where I work, that studio is my baby. I work my day job for the Illinois Press Association from 8 AM to 5 PM as their graphic designer, then I head over to the shop and start my evening, tattooing, talking to clients, doing touch-ups, consults, just about whatever I can accomplish until 8 PM.

On Saturdays, I am at the shop from noon to 8 PM. This is the time I enjoy the most. Sitting down in front of a client with my machine ready to go is such a stress reliever for me. Once I get going on the piece, I am as calm as can be, and nothing in the world can bother me. It is hard to remember to take breaks when I am working on large pieces. I always have to remind myself.

I know my father is proud of me, and that means the world to me. I strive every day to be the best artist I can. I just wish there were more hours in a day! I never have enough time to get everything done.

As a woman, working in the tattoo industry, you have to have a thick skin. Especially in small towns, where every tattoo artist knows you. I have learned how to deal with gossip, rumors and "under-the-table talk." Basically it goes in one ear, and out the other. I don't stoop to that level; it is a waste of time. The best representation of a good tattoo artist is the word of mouth from his or her clients. A satisfied customer is the best advertising!

I hang the ego at the door and make sure that every client that I work with is 100% satisfied. And I make sure that I am as accessible as possible for my clients. Clients in the tattoo industry don't just stay clients, they become good friends, and when they pop into the shop just to chat or show me their tattoo, it makes it all worth it. I would not change my life for anything . . . well, maybe more money. I seem to have a conscience and I always underprice myself.

Slowing Down Is a Revelation

I have come to a revelation! I have learned that you cannot rush a piece of art. When I have had to rush on a tattoo design or the actual tattoo, I can see what I would have changed after I get the photos of the tattoos back.

Granted, my clients love the work, and come back for more, but I see the potential the work I could have had if I would have spent more time on it and if price was not an issue. I have a lot of clients that are impatient or on a deadline, or on a tight budget, so I have had to bend myself over backwards to meet those needs of each client, and it does affect the outcome of the whole design, let alone my stress level.

So now after thinking about it long and hard, I have changed a couple of things. . . . First I am going to keep both my careers for now, Tattooing and Graphic Design. I love both my jobs. I believe that if I control the scheduling a little better, and limit the stress of having to rush everything, my tattoo works of art will be better than ever. This means that my clients will have to work with me on my schedule and in some cases it may be 2–8 weeks before you can get in, but if you look around, that is usually the average waiting period for an artist.

A Tattoo Is for the Rest of Your Life

If a client works with me, and we design a tattoo that is a work of art instead of just a cover up or just a kanji [Japanese or Chinese characters], I know that the client will like it more and respect the fact that they will be wearing it for the rest of their life and appreciate the artistic aspect of it. PLUS they will know that I put my heart and soul into it and did not rush.

I have learned a lot by speaking to my tattoo peers from around the country, and to become the artist that I have always dreamed of, I need to slow down and take more time on each tattoo design and with each client. I do not want to just hammer out tattoos all day, I want to create award-winning pieces of art that my clients will wear proudly and will come to appreciate the process of how we got there and how much the designs affect their life, especially if it is a sentimental piece of art that is close to their heart.

Organizations to Contact

The editors have compiled the following list of organizations concerned with the issues debated in this book. The descriptions are derived from materials provided by the organizations. All have publications or information available for interested readers. The list was compiled on the date of publication of the present volume; the information provided here may change. Be aware that many organizations take several weeks or longer to respond to inquiries, so allow as much time as possible.

Alliance of Professional Tattooists (APT)
9210 S. Highway 17-92, Maitland, FL   32751
(407) 831-5549
Web site: www.safe-tattoos.com

The APT is a nonprofit educational organization that was founded in 1992 to address the health and safety issues facing the tattoo industry. The organization seeks to dispel myths and misconceptions surrounding tattooing through education and awareness and holds seminars on disease prevention at tattoo conventions across the United States. The organization provides advice and news on its Web site.

Association of Professional Piercers (APP)
P.O. Box 1287, Lawrence, KS   66044
(785) 841-6060
Web site: www.safepiercing.org

The APP is an international nonprofit association dedicated to the dissemination of vital health and safety information related to body piercings, piercers, health care providers, and the general public. The Web site features frequently asked questions about piercing, guidelines on selecting a safe piercer, and links to information on anatomy and infection control.

Centers for Disease Control and Prevention (CDC)
1600 Clifton Road, Atlanta, GA   30333
(404) 498-1515
Web site: www.cdc.gov

The Centers for Disease Control and Prevention (CDC), a part of the U.S. Department of Health and Human Services, is the primary federal agency for conducting and supporting public health activities in the United States. CDC publishes many articles, news, and fact sheets online, including information for both body artists and consumers considering tattoos and piercing.

Empire State Tattoo Club of America (ESTCA)
P.O. Box 1374, Mount Vernon, NY   10550
(914) 664-9894 • fax: (914) 668-5200

ESTCA is an international organization of tattoo artists and individuals with tattoos. It works to increase public awareness of tattoo art and sponsors competitions and bestows awards.

National Tattoo Association (NTA)
485 Business Park Lane, Allentown, PA   18109
(215) 433-7261 • fax: (215) 433-7294
Web site: www.nationaltattooassociation.com

The NTA was founded in 1974; its members include tattoo artists and enthusiasts. The organization promotes tattooing as a viable contemporary art form and seeks to upgrade standards and practices of tattooing. Industry news is posted on its Web site.

Tattoo Club of America (TCA)
c/o Spider Webb's Studio, Captains Cove Seaport
1 Bastwick Avenue, Bridgeport, CT   06605
(203) 335-3992

The TCA welcomes tattoo artists and individuals worldwide who have been tattooed. It promotes the art of tattooing and seeks to make it more acceptable to the general public. TCA publishes a quarterly newsletter and holds an annual convention in New York City.

For Further Research

Books

Jane Caplan, *Written on the Body: The Tattoo in European and American History*. Princeton, NJ: Princeton University Press, 2000.

Dale Durfee, *Tattoo*. Atglen, PA: Schiffer, 2000.

Mike Featherstone, *Body Modification*. Thousand Oaks, CA: Sage, 2000.

Fiona Gardner, *Self-Harm: A Psychotherapeutic Approach*. New York: Brunner-Routledge, 2001.

Ariel Glucklich, *Sacred Pain: Hurting the Body for the Sake of the Soul*. New York: Oxford University Press, 2001.

Ruth Holliday and John Hassard, *Contested Bodies*. New York: Routledge, 2001.

Mira Kamdar, *Motiba's Tattoos: A Granddaughter's Journey into Her Indian Family's Past*. New York: PublicAffairs, 2000.

Michelle Keown, *Postcolonial Pacific Writing: Representations of the Body*. New York: Routledge, 2005.

Takahiro Kitamura, *Bushido: Legacies of the Japanese Tattoo*. Atglen, PA: Schiffer, 2000.

Sue Nicholson, *Body Art*. Philadelphia: Running Press, 2001.

Sarah M. Pike, *Earthly Bodies, Magical Selves: Contemporary Pagans and the Search for Community*. Berkeley: University of California Press, 2001.

Bradley Quinn, *Techno Fashion*. Oxford, UK: Berg, 2002.

Burkhard Riemschneider, *1000 Tattoos*. Los Angeles: Taschen, 2005.

Spider Webb, *The Great Book of Tattoo*. Atglen, PA: Schiffer, 2002.

Periodicals

Myrna L. Armstrong, "Tattooing, Body Piercing, and Permanent Cosmetics: A Historical and Current View of State Regulations, with Continuing Concerns," *Journal of Environmental Health*, April 2005.

Michael Atkinson, "Tattooing and Civilizing Processes: Body Modification as Self-Control," *Canadian Review of Sociology and Anthropology*, May 2004.

Jenny Balfour-Paul, "Exuberant Dress, Extraordinary Tattoos," *Geographical*, November 2006.

Lynne Carroll and Roxanne Anderson, "Body Piercing, Tattooing, Self-Esteem, and Body Investment in Adolescent Girls," *Adolescence*, 2002.

Beth Felker Jones, "Marked for Life," *Christian Century*, May 2007.

Haidy Geismar, "Tattoo: Bodies, Art, and Exchange in the Pacific and the West," *Pacific Affairs*, 2005.

Daina Hawkes, Charlene Y. Senn, and Chantal Thorn, "Factors That Influence Attitudes Toward Women with Tattoos," *Sex Roles: A Journal of Research*, 2004.

Tim Keel, "Tattooed: Body Art Goes Mainstream," *Christian Century*, May 2007.

Joy Bennett Kinnon, "Pierced to Death," *Ebony*, April 2000.

Andres Martin, "On Teenagers and Tattoos," *Reclaiming Children and Youth*, Fall 2000.

Victoria McGovern, "Tattoos: Safe Symbols?" *Environmental Health Perspectives*, September 2005.

Paul Miles, "Bodies to Dye For," *Geographical*, October 2001.

William Riley, "Interpreting Gang Tattoos," *Corrections Today*, April 2006.

John Senz, "Tattoo Cool," *School Arts*, February 2005.

Nick Smith, "Symbols in the Skin," *Geographical*, April 2007.

Wendy Strauch-Nelson, "Facing Up to Body Art: 'As Soon as I Turn Eighteen, I'm Getting a Tattoo,'" *School Arts*, September 2004.

Ken Vieth, "To Tattoo or Not to Tattoo? . . . Is That Really the Question?" *School Arts*, May–June 2006.

Index

Tattooing
churches and, 12–14
collaborative, 64, 66
employers and, 35, 50
as heritage reconnection, 27–30
in Japan, 35
pain in, 34, 36, 55
recovery from, 41–44
Tattoos
as art, 27–31, 60–67
designs, 30, 33–38, 48, 49, 55, 56
as life story, 33–35
reasons for having, 36–38
removal, 50–54, 58
Tedder, Dave, 65, 66, 67
Teenage body piercing, 22–26
See also Body piercing
Temple Beth Shalom (Roslyn Heights, NY), 13
Texas Instruments, 73
Titanium plugs/eyelets, 76

Tongue piercing, 45–48
Toronto (ON), 45, 48
Toughness, 56
222 Tattoo (San Francisco), 60
Tylenol, 47

V

Ventura (CA), 69
Vicodin, 36
Voltron, 67

W

"Warlord Kitty," 68
Waulken, Joe, 65, 67
Weatherholtz, Justin, 67
Wheel of Fortune (TV show), 38
Whore (Bond), 62–63
Woodkowski, Josh, 65, 66

Y

Yount, Jack, 80